Aristotle

A Biography

Editor

Devin Bays

Scribbles

Year of Publication 2018

ISBN : 9789352979646

Book Published by

Scribbles

(An Imprint of Alpha Editions)

email - alphaedis@gmail.com

Produced by: PediaPress GmbH
Limburg an der Lahn
Germany
http://pediapress.com/

The content within this book was generated collaboratively by volunteers. Please be advised that nothing found here has necessarily been reviewed by people with the expertise required to provide you with complete, accurate or reliable information. Some information in this book may be misleading or simply wrong. Alpha Editions and PediaPress does not guarantee the validity of the information found here. If you need specific advice (for example, medical, legal, financial, or risk management) please seek a professional who is licensed or knowledgeable in that area.

Sources, licenses and contributors of the articles and images are listed in the section entitled "References". Parts of the books may be licensed under the GNU Free Documentation License. A copy of this license is included in the section entitled "GNU Free Documentation License"

The views and characters expressed in the book are those of the contributors and his/her imagination and do not represent the views of the Publisher.

Contents

Articles   **1**

    Aristotle 1

Appendix   **49**

    References 49

    Article Sources and Contributors 53

    Image Sources, Licenses and Contributors 54

Article Licenses   **55**

Index   **57**

Aristotle

<indicator name="pp-default"> 🔒 </indicator> <indicator name="good-star"> ⊕ </indicator>

Aristotle	
 Roman copy in marble of a Greek bronze bust of Aristotle by Lysippos, c. 330 BC, with modern alabaster mantle	
Born	384 BC Stagira, Chalkidiki, Chalcidian League, Northern Greece
Died	322 BC (aged approx. 62) Euboea, Greece, Macedonian Empire
Era	Ancient philosophy
Region	Western philosophy
School	• Peripatetic school • Aristotelianism
Main interests	• Biology • Zoology • Psychology[1] • Physics • Metaphysics • Logic • Ethics • Rhetoric • Music • Poetry • Economics • Politics • Government

Notable ideas	• Aristotelian philosophy • Syllogism • Theory of the soul • Virtue ethics

Aristotle (/ˈærɪˌstɒtəl/;[2] Greek: Ἀριστοτέλης *Aristotélēs*, pronounced [aristotélɛːs]; 384–322 BC)[3] was an ancient Greek philosopher and scientist born in the city of Stagira, Chalkidiki, in the north of Classical Greece. Along with Plato, Aristotle is considered the "Father of Western Philosophy", which inherited almost its entire lexicon from his teachings, including problems and methods of inquiry, so influencing almost all forms of knowledge known to the West.

Little is known for certain about his life. His father, Nicomachus, died when Aristotle was a child, and he was brought up by a guardian. At seventeen or eighteen years of age, he joined Plato's Academy in Athens and remained there until the age of thirty-seven (c. 347 BC). His writings cover many subjects – including physics, biology, zoology, metaphysics, logic, ethics, aesthetics, poetry, theatre, music, rhetoric, psychology, linguistics, economics, politics and government – and constitute the first comprehensive system of Western philosophy. Shortly after Plato died, Aristotle left Athens and, at the request of Philip II of Macedon, tutored Alexander the Great beginning in 343 BC.[4] Teaching Alexander gave Aristotle many opportunities. He established a library in the Lyceum which helped him to produce many of his hundreds of books, which were papyrus scrolls. The fact that Aristotle was a pupil of Plato contributed to his former views of Platonism, but, following Plato's death, Aristotle immersed himself in empirical studies and shifted from Platonism to empiricism.[5] He believed all concepts and knowledge were ultimately based on perception. Aristotle's views on natural sciences represent the groundwork underlying many of his works.

Aristotle's views on physical science profoundly shaped medieval scholarship. Their influence extended from Late Antiquity and the Early Middle Ages into the Renaissance, and were not replaced systematically until the Enlightenment and theories such as classical mechanics. Some of Aristotle's zoological observations, such as on the hectocotyl (reproductive) arm of the octopus, were disbelieved until the 19th century. His works contain the earliest known formal study of logic, studied by medieval scholars such as Peter Abelard and John Buridan. Aristotelianism profoundly influenced Islamic thought during the Middle Ages, as well as Christian theology, especially the Neoplatonism of the Early Church and the scholastic tradition of the Catholic Church. Aristotle was revered among medieval Muslim scholars as "The First Teacher". His ethics, though always influential, gained renewed interest with the modern advent of virtue ethics.

Figure 1: *School of Aristotle in Mieza, Macedonia, Greece*

All aspects of Aristotle's philosophy continue to be the object of academic study. Though Aristotle wrote many elegant treatises and dialogues for publication, only around a third of his original output has survived, none of it intended for publication.[6] Aristotle has been depicted by major artists including Raphael and Rembrandt. Early Modern theories including William Harvey's circulation of the blood and Galileo Galilei's kinematics were developed in reaction to Aristotle's. In the 19th century, George Boole gave Aristotle's logic a mathematical foundation with his system of algebraic logic. In the 20th century, Martin Heidegger created a new interpretation of Aristotle's political philosophy, but elsewhere Aristotle was widely criticised, even ridiculed by thinkers such as the philosopher Bertrand Russell and the biologist Peter Medawar.[7] More recently, Aristotle has again been taken seriously, such as in the thinking of Ayn Rand and Alasdair MacIntyre, while Armand Marie Leroi has reconstructed Aristotle's biology. The image of Aristotle tutoring the young Alexander remains current, and the *Poetics* continues to play a role in the cinema of the United States.

Life

In general, the details of Aristotle's life are not well-established. The biographies written in ancient times are often speculative and historians only agree on a few salient points.[8]

Aristotle, whose name means "the best purpose" in Ancient Greek, was born in 384 BC in Stagira, Chalcidice, about 55 km (34 miles) east of modern-day Thessaloniki. His father Nicomachus was the personal physician to King Amyntas of Macedon. Both of Aristotle's parents died when he was about thirteen, and Proxenus of Atarneus became his guardian. Although little information about Aristotle's childhood has survived, he probably spent some time within the Macedonian palace, making his first connections with the Macedonian monarchy.

At the age of seventeen or eighteen, Aristotle moved to Athens to continue his education at Plato's Academy. He remained there for nearly twenty years before leaving Athens in 348/47 BC. The traditional story about his departure records that he was disappointed with the Academy's direction after control passed to Plato's nephew Speusippus, although it is possible that he feared the anti-Macedonian sentiments in Athens at that time and left before Plato died. Aristotle then accompanied Xenocrates to the court of his friend Hermias of Atarneus in Asia Minor. After the death of Hermias, Aristotle travelled with his pupil Theophrastus to the island of Lesbos, where together they researched the botany and zoology of the island and its sheltered lagoon. While in Lesbos, Aristotle married Pythias, either Hermias's adoptive daughter or niece. She bore him a daughter, whom they also named Pythias. In 343 BC, Aristotle was invited by Philip II of Macedon to become the tutor to his son Alexander.

Aristotle was appointed as the head of the royal academy of Macedon. During Aristotle's time in the Macedonian court, he gave lessons not only to Alexander, but also to two other future kings: Ptolemy and Cassander. Aristotle encouraged Alexander toward eastern conquest and Aristotle's own attitude towards Persia was unabashedly ethnocentric. In one famous example, he counsels Alexander to be "a leader to the Greeks and a despot to the barbarians, to look after the former as after friends and relatives, and to deal with the latter as with beasts or plants". By 335 BC, Aristotle had returned to Athens, establishing his own school there known as the Lyceum. Aristotle conducted courses at the school for the next twelve years. While in Athens, his wife Pythias died and Aristotle became involved with Herpyllis of Stagira, who bore him a son whom he named after his father, Nicomachus. According to the *Suda*, he also had an *erômenos*, Palaephatus of Abydus.[9]

This period in Athens, between 335 and 323 BC, is when Aristotle is believed to have composed many of his works. He wrote many dialogues, of which only fragments have survived. Those works that have survived are in treatise form and were not, for the most part, intended for widespread publication; they are generally thought to be lecture aids for his students. His most important treatises include *Physics*, *Metaphysics*, *Nicomachean Ethics*, *Politics*, *On the Soul* and *Poetics*. Aristotle studied and made significant contributions

Figure 2: *Portrait bust of Aristotle; an Imperial Roman (1st or 2nd century AD) copy of a lost bronze sculpture made by Lysippos*

to "logic, metaphysics, mathematics, physics, biology, botany, ethics, politics, agriculture, medicine, dance and theatre."

Near the end of his life, Alexander and Aristotle became estranged over Alexander's relationship with Persia and Persians. A widespread tradition in antiquity suspected Aristotle of playing a role in Alexander's death, but the only evidence of this is an unlikely claim made some six years after the death. Following Alexander's death, anti-Macedonian sentiment in Athens was rekindled. In 322 BC, Demophilus and Eurymedon the Hierophant reportedly denounced Aristotle for impiety, prompting him to flee to his mother's family estate in Chalcis, on Euboea, at which occasion he was said to have stated: "I will not allow the Athenians to sin twice against philosophy"[10] – a reference to Athens's trial and execution of Socrates. He died on Euboea of natural causes later that same year, having named his student Antipater as his chief executor and leaving a will in which he asked to be buried next to his wife.

Abstract philosophy

Logic

With the *Prior Analytics*, Aristotle is credited with the earliest study of formal logic, and his conception of it was the dominant form of Western logic until 19th-century advances in mathematical logic. Kant stated in the *Critique of Pure Reason* that with Aristotle logic reached its completion.

Analytics and the *Organon*

One of Aristotle's types of syllogism[11]

In words	In terms[12]	In equations[13] </ref>
All men are mortal. All Greeks are men. ∴ All Greeks are mortal.	M a P S a M S a P	$\overline{\exists x: M_x \wedge \overline{P_x}}$ $\wedge\ \overline{\exists x:\ S_x \wedge \overline{M_x}}$ $\Rightarrow \overline{\exists x:\ S_x \wedge \overline{P_x}}$

What we today call *Aristotelian logic* with its types of syllogism (methods of logical argument), Aristotle himself would have labelled "analytics". The term "logic" he reserved to mean *dialectics*. Most of Aristotle's work is probably not in its original form, because it was most likely edited by students and later lecturers. The logical works of Aristotle were compiled into a set of six books called the *Organon* around 40 BC by Andronicus of Rhodes or others among his followers. The books are:

1. *Categories*
2. *On Interpretation*
3. *Prior Analytics*
4. *Posterior Analytics*
5. *Topics*
6. *On Sophistical Refutations*

The order of the books (or the teachings from which they are composed) is not certain, but this list was derived from analysis of Aristotle's writings. It goes from the basics, the analysis of simple terms in the *Categories,* the analysis of propositions and their elementary relations in *On Interpretation*, to the study of more complex forms, namely, syllogisms (in the *Analytics*)[14] and dialectics (in the *Topics* and *Sophistical Refutations*). The first three treatises form the core of the logical theory *stricto sensu*: the grammar of the language of logic and the correct rules of reasoning. The *Rhetoric* is not conventionally included, but it states that it relies on the *Topics*.

Figure 3: *Plato (left) and Aristotle in Raphael's 1509 fresco, The School of Athens. Aristotle holds his Nicomachean Ethics and gestures to the earth, representing empirical observation, whilst Plato gestures to the heavens, representing The Forms, and holds his Timaeus.*

Epistemology

Like his teacher Plato, Aristotle's philosophy aims at the universal. Aristotle's ontology places the universal (*katholou*) in particulars (*kath' hekaston*), things in the world, whereas for Plato the universal is a separately existing form which actual things imitate. This means that Aristotle's epistemology is based on the study of things that exist or happen in the world, and rises to knowledge of the universal, whereas for Plato epistemology begins with knowledge of universal Forms (or ideas) and descends to knowledge of particular imitations of these. For Aristotle, "form" is still what phenomena are based on, but is "instantiated" in a particular substance. Aristotle uses induction from examples alongside deduction, whereas Plato relies on deduction from *a priori* principles.

In Aristotle's terminology, "natural philosophy" is a branch of philosophy examining the phenomena of the natural world, and includes fields that would be regarded today as physics, biology and other natural sciences. Aristotle's work encompassed virtually all facets of intellectual inquiry. Aristotle makes philosophy in the broad sense coextensive with reasoning, which he also would describe as "science". Note, however, that his use of the term *science* carries a different meaning than that covered by the term "scientific method". For Aristotle, "all science (*dianoia*) is either practical, poetical or theoretical" (*Metaphysics* 1025b25). His practical science includes ethics and politics; his poetical science means the study of fine arts including poetry; his theoretical science covers physics, mathematics and metaphysics.

Metaphysics

Aristotle coined the term "metaphysics". He also called it "first philosophy", and distinguished it from mathematics and natural science (physics) as the contemplative (*theoretikē*) philosophy which is "theological" and studies the divine. He wrote in his *Metaphysics* (1026a16):

> if there were no other independent things besides the composite natural ones, the study of nature would be the primary kind of knowledge; but if there is some motionless independent thing, the knowledge of this precedes it and is first philosophy, and it is universal *in just this way*, because it is first. And it belongs to this sort of philosophy to study being as being, both what it is and what belongs to it just by virtue of being.

Substance, potentiality and actuality

Aristotle examines the concepts of substance (*ousia*) and essence (*to ti ên einai*, "the what it was to be") in his *Metaphysics* (Book VII), and he concludes that a particular substance is a combination of both matter and form, a philosophical theory called hylomorphism. In Book VIII, he distinguishes the matter of the substance as the substratum, or the stuff of which it is composed. For example, the matter of a house is the bricks, stones, timbers etc., or whatever constitutes the *potential* house, while the form of the substance is the *actual* house, namely 'covering for bodies and chattels' or any other differentia that let us define something as a house. The formula that gives the components is the account of the matter, and the formula that gives the differentia is the account of the form.[15]

With regard to the change (*kinesis*) and its causes now, as he defines in his *Physics* and *On Generation and Corruption* 319b–320a, he distinguishes the coming to be from:

1. growth and diminution, which is change in quantity;
2. locomotion, which is change in space; and
3. alteration, which is change in quality.

Figure 4: *Aristotle argued that a capability like playing the flute could be acquired – the potential made actual – by learning.*

The coming to be is a change where nothing persists of which the resultant is a property. In that particular change he introduces the concept of potentiality (*dynamis*) and actuality (*entelecheia*) in association with the matter and the form. Referring to potentiality, this is what a thing is capable of doing, or being acted upon, if the conditions are right and it is not prevented by something else. For example, the seed of a plant in the soil is potentially (*dynamei*) plant, and if is not prevented by something, it will become a plant. Potentially beings can either 'act' (*poiein*) or 'be acted upon' (*paschein*), which can be either innate or learned. For example, the eyes possess the potentiality of sight (innate – being acted upon), while the capability of playing the flute can be possessed by learning (exercise – acting). Actuality is the fulfilment of the end of the potentiality. Because the end (*telos*) is the principle of every change, and for the sake of the end exists potentiality, therefore actuality is the end. Referring then to our previous example, we could say that an actuality is when a plant does one of the activities that plants do.

> *For that for the sake of which (to hou heneka) a thing is, is its principle, and the becoming is for the sake of the end; and the actuality is the end, and it is for the sake of this that the potentiality is acquired. For animals do not see in order that they may have sight, but they have sight that they may see.*[16]

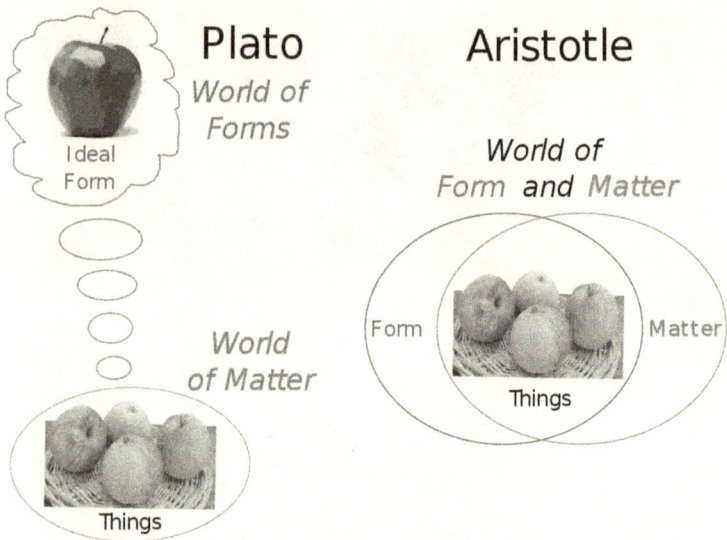

Figure 5: *Plato's forms exist as universals, like the ideal form of an apple. For Aristotle, both matter and form belong to the individual thing (hylomorphism).*

In summary, the matter used to make a house has potentiality to be a house and both the activity of building and the form of the final house are actualities, which is also a final cause or end. Then Aristotle proceeds and concludes that the actuality is prior to potentiality in formula, in time and in substantiality. With this definition of the particular substance (i.e., matter and form), Aristotle tries to solve the problem of the unity of the beings, for example, "what is it that makes a man one"? Since, according to Plato there are two Ideas: animal and biped, how then is man a unity? However, according to Aristotle, the potential being (matter) and the actual one (form) are one and the same.[17]

Universals and particulars

Plato argued that all things have a universal form, which could be either a property or a relation to other things. When we look at an apple, for example, we see an apple, and we can also analyse a form of an apple. In this distinction, there is a particular apple and a universal form of an apple. Moreover, we can place an apple next to a book, so that we can speak of both the book and apple as being next to each other. Plato argued that there are some universal forms that are not a part of particular things. For example, it is possible that there is no particular good in existence, but "good" is still a proper universal form. Aristotle disagreed with Plato on this point, arguing that all universals are instantiated at some period of time, and that there are no universals that

Figure 6: *The four classical elements (fire, air, water, earth) of Empedocles and Aristotle illustrated with a burning log. The log releases all four elements as it is destroyed.*

are unattached to existing things. In addition, Aristotle disagreed with Plato about the location of universals. Where Plato spoke of the world of forms, a place where all universal forms subsist, Aristotle maintained that universals exist within each thing on which each universal is predicated. So, according to Aristotle, the form of apple exists within each apple, rather than in the world of the forms.[18]

Natural philosophy

Aristotle's "natural philosophy" spans a wide range of natural phenomena including those now covered by physics, biology and other natural sciences.

Physics

Five elements

In his *On Generation and Corruption*, Aristotle related each of the four elements proposed earlier by Empedocles, Earth, Water, Air, and Fire, to two of the four sensible qualities, hot, cold, wet, and dry. In the Empedoclean scheme, all matter was made of the four elements, in differing proportions.

Aristotle's scheme added the heavenly Aether, the divine substance of the heavenly spheres, stars and planets.[19]

Aristotle's elements[19]

Element	Hot/Cold	Wet/Dry	Motion	Modern state of matter
Earth	Cold	Dry	Down	Solid
Water	Cold	Wet	Down	Liquid
Air	Hot	Wet	Up	Gas
Fire	Hot	Dry	Up	Plasma
Aether	(divine substance)	—	Circular (in heavens)	—

Motion

Aristotle describes two kinds of motion: "violent" or "unnatural motion", such as that of a thrown stone, in the *Physics* (254b10), and "natural motion", such as of a falling object, in *On the Heavens* (300a20). In violent motion, as soon as the agent stops causing it, the motion stops also; in other words, the natural state of an object is to be at rest,[20] since Aristotle does not address friction. With this understanding, it can be observed that, as Aristotle stated, heavy objects (on the ground, say) require more force to make them move; and objects pushed with greater force move faster.[21] This would imply the equation

$$F = mv,$$

However, in modern physics this was proved to be incorrect.

Natural motion depends on the element concerned: the aether naturally moves in a circle around the heavens,[22]</ref> while the 4 Empedoclean elements move vertically up (like fire, as is observed) or down (like earth) towards their natural resting places.[23]

In the *Physics* (215a25), Aristotle effectively states a quantitative law, that the speed, v, of a falling body is proportional (say, with constant c) to its weight, W, and inversely proportional to the density,[24] ρ, of the fluid in which it is falling:

$$v = c\frac{W}{\rho}$$

Aristotle implies that in a vacuum the speed of fall would become infinite, and concludes from this apparent absurdity that a vacuum is not possible. Opinions have varied on whether Aristotle intended to state quantitative laws. Henri

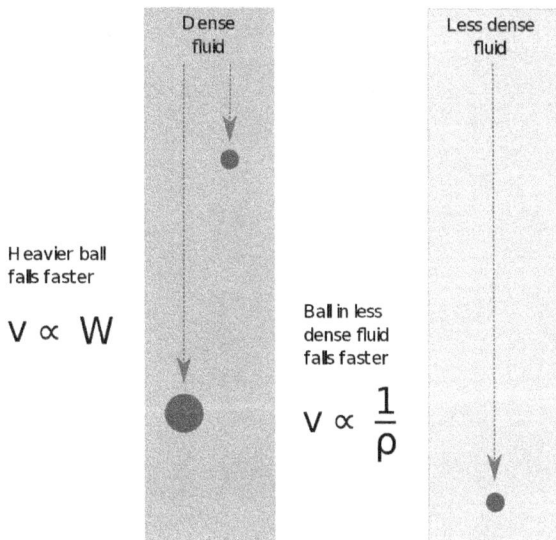

Figure 7: *Aristotle's laws of motion. In Physics he states that objects fall at a speed proportional to their weight and inversely proportional to the density of the fluid they are immersed in. This is a correct approximation for objects in Earth's gravitational field moving in air or water.*

Carteron held the "extreme view" that Aristotle's concept of force was basically qualitative, but other authors reject this.

Archimedes corrected Aristotle's theory that bodies move towards their natural resting places; metal boats can float if they displace enough water; floating depends in Archimedes' scheme on the mass and volume of the object, not as Aristotle thought its elementary composition.

Aristotle's writings on motion remained influential until the Early Modern period. John Philoponus (in the Middle Ages) and Galileo are said to have shown by experiment that Aristotle's claim that a heavier object falls faster than a lighter object is incorrect. A contrary opinion is given by Carlo Rovelli, who argues that Aristotle's physics of motion is correct within its domain of validity, that of objects in the Earth's gravitational field immersed in a fluid such as air. In this system, heavy bodies in steady fall indeed travel faster than light ones (whether friction is ignored, or not), and they do fall more slowly in a denser medium.[25]

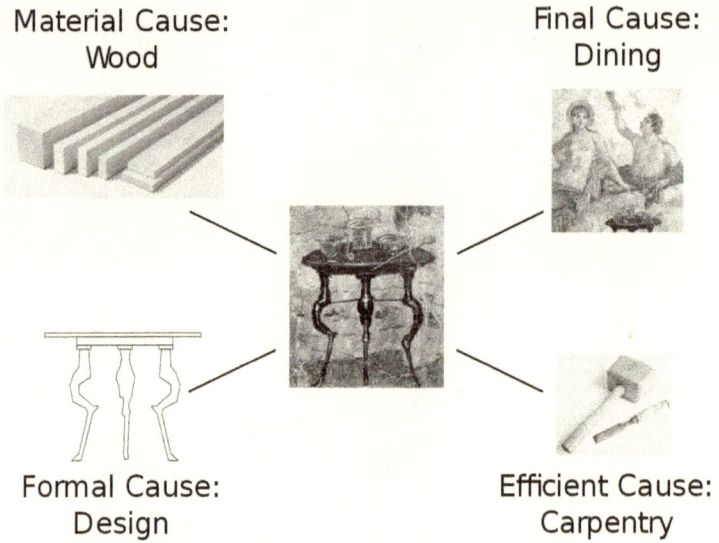

Figure 8: *Aristotle argued by analogy with woodwork that a thing takes its form from four causes: in the case of a table, the wood used (material cause), its design (formal cause), the tools and techniques used (efficient cause), and its decorative or practical purpose (final cause).*[26]

Newton's "forced" motion corresponds to Aristotle's "violent" motion with its external agent, but Aristotle's assumption that the agent's effect stops immediately it stops acting (e.g., the ball leaves the thrower's hand) has awkward consequences: he has to suppose that surrounding fluid helps to push the ball along to make it continue to rise even though the hand is no longer acting on it, resulting in the Medieval theory of impetus.

Four causes

Aristotle suggested that the reason for anything coming about can be attributed to four different types of simultaneously active factors. His term *aitia* is traditionally translated as "cause", but it does not always refer to temporal sequence; it might be better translated as "explanation", but the traditional rendering will be employed here.

- Material cause describes the material out of which something is composed. Thus the material cause of a table is wood. It is not about action. It does not mean that one domino knocks over another domino.

- The formal cause is its form, i.e., the arrangement of that matter. It tells us what a thing is, that a thing is determined by the definition, form, pattern, essence, whole, synthesis or archetype. It embraces the account of causes in terms of fundamental principles or general laws, as the whole (i.e., macrostructure) is the cause of its parts, a relationship known as the whole-part causation. Plainly put, the formal cause is the idea in the mind of the sculptor that brings the sculpture into being. A simple example of the formal cause is the mental image or idea that allows an artist, architect, or engineer to create a drawing.
- The efficient cause is "the primary source", or that from which the change under consideration proceeds. It identifies 'what makes of what is made and what causes change of what is changed' and so suggests all sorts of agents, nonliving or living, acting as the sources of change or movement or rest. Representing the current understanding of causality as the relation of cause and effect, this covers the modern definitions of "cause" as either the agent or agency or particular events or states of affairs. In the case of two dominoes, when the first is knocked over it causes the second also to fall over. In the case of animals, this agency is a combination of how it develops from the egg, and how its body functions.[27]
- The final cause (*telos*) is its purpose, the reason why a thing exists or is done, including both purposeful and instrumental actions and activities. The final cause is the purpose or function that something is supposed to serve. This covers modern ideas of motivating causes, such as volition. In the case of living things, it implies adaptation to a particular way of life.[27]

Optics

Aristotle describes experiments in optics using a camera obscura in *Problems*, book 15. The apparatus consisted of a dark chamber with a small aperture that let light in. With it, he saw that whatever shape he made the hole, the sun's image always remained circular. He also noted that increasing the distance between the aperture and the image surface magnified the image.

Chance and spontaneity

According to Aristotle, spontaneity and chance are causes of some things, distinguishable from other types of cause such as simple necessity. Chance as an incidental cause lies in the realm of accidental things, "from what is spontaneous". There is also more a specific kind of chance, which Aristotle names "luck", that only applies to people's moral choices.[28]

Figure 9: *Aristotle noted that the ground level of the Aeolian islands changed before a volcanic eruption.*

Astronomy

In astronomy, Aristotle refuted Democritus's claim that the Milky Way was made up of "those stars which are shaded by the earth from the sun's rays," pointing out correctly that if "the size of the sun is greater than that of the earth and the distance of the stars from the earth many times greater than that of the sun, then... the sun shines on all the stars and the earth screens none of them."[29]

Geology

Aristotle was one of the first people to record any geological observations. He stated that geological change was too slow to be observed in one person's lifetime.[30] The geologist Charles Lyell noted that Aristotle described such change, including "lakes that had dried up" and "deserts that had become watered by rivers", giving as examples the growth of the Nile delta since the time of Homer, and "the upheaving of one of the Aeolian islands, previous to a volcanic eruption."'

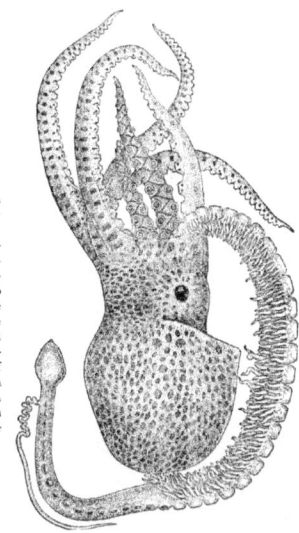

Figure 10: *Among many pioneering zoological observations, Aristotle described the reproductive hectocotyl arm of the octopus (bottom left).*

Biology

Empirical research

Aristotle was the first person to study biology systematically,[31] and biology forms a large part of his writings. He spent two years observing and describing the zoology of Lesbos and the surrounding seas, including in particular the Pyrrha lagoon in the centre of Lesbos.[32] His data in *History of Animals, Generation of Animals, Movement of Animals*, and *Parts of Animals* are assembled from his own observations, statements given by people with specialised knowledge such as beekeepers and fishermen, and less accurate accounts provided by travellers from overseas.[33] His apparent emphasis on animals rather than plants is a historical accident: his works on botany have been lost, but two books on plants by his pupil Theophrastus have survived.

Aristotle reports on the sea-life visible from observation on Lesbos and the catches of fishermen. He describes the catfish, electric ray, and frogfish in detail, as well as cephalopods such as the octopus and paper nautilus. His description of the hectocotyl arm of cephalopods, used in sexual reproduction, was widely disbelieved until the 19th century.[34] He gives accurate descriptions of the four-chambered fore-stomachs of ruminants,[35] and of the ovoviviparous embryological development of the hound shark.[36]

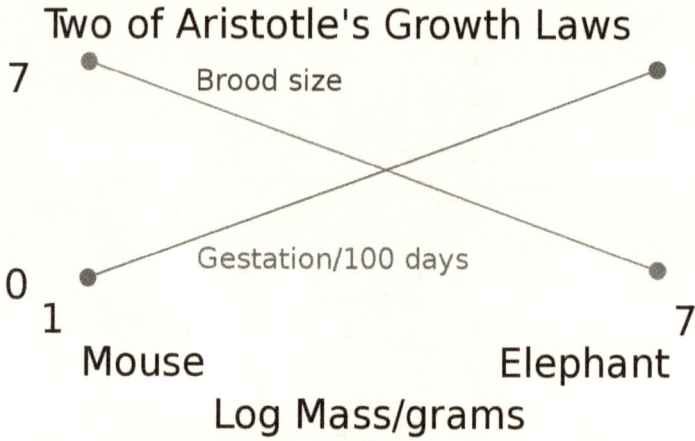

Figure 11: *Aristotle inferred growth laws from his observations on animals, including that brood size decreases with body mass, whereas gestation period increases. He was correct in these predictions, at least for mammals: data are shown for mouse and elephant.*

He notes that an animal's structure is well matched to function, so, among birds, the heron, which lives in marshes with soft mud and lives by catching fish, has a long neck and long legs, and a sharp spear-like beak, whereas ducks that swim have short legs and webbed feet.[37] Darwin, too, noted these sorts of differences between similar kinds of animal, but unlike Aristotle used the data to come to the theory of evolution.[38] Aristotle's writings can seem to modern readers close to implying evolution, but while Aristotle was aware that new mutations or hybridisations could occur, he saw these as rare accidents. For Aristotle, accidents, like heat waves in winter, must be considered distinct from natural causes. He was thus critical of Empedocles's materialist theory of a "survival of the fittest" origin of living things and their organs, and ridiculed the idea that accidents could lead to orderly results. To put his views into modern terms, he nowhere says that different species can have a common ancestor, or that one kind can change into another, or that kinds can become extinct.[39]

Scientific style

Aristotle did not do experiments in the modern sense.[40] He used the ancient Greek term *pepeiramenoi* to mean observations, or at most investigative procedures like dissection.[41] In *Generation of Animals*, he finds a fertilised hen's egg of a suitable stage and opens it to see the embryo's heart beating inside.[42]

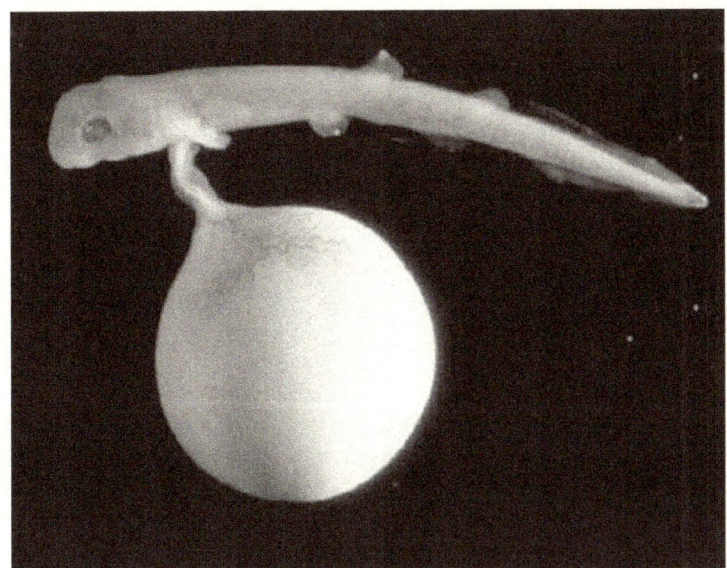

Figure 12: *Aristotle recorded that the embryo of a dogfish was attached by a cord to a kind of placenta (the yolk sac), like a higher animal; this formed an exception to the linear scale from highest to lowest.*[46]

Instead, he practised a different style of science: systematically gathering data, discovering patterns common to whole groups of animals, and inferring possible causal explanations from these.[43,44] This style is common in modern biology when large amounts of data become available in a new field, such as genomics. It does not result in the same certainty as experimental science, but it sets out testable hypotheses and constructs a narrative explanation of what is observed. In this sense, Aristotle's biology is scientific.[43]

From the data he collected and documented, Aristotle inferred quite a number of rules relating the life-history features of the live-bearing tetrapods (terrestrial placental mammals) that he studied. Among these correct predictions are the following. Brood size decreases with (adult) body mass, so that an elephant has fewer young (usually just one) per brood than a mouse. Lifespan increases with gestation period, and also with body mass, so that elephants live longer than mice, have a longer period of gestation, and are heavier. As a final example, fecundity decreases with lifespan, so long-lived kinds like elephants have fewer young in total than short-lived kinds like mice.[45]

Classification of living things

Aristotle distinguished about 500 species of animals, arranging these in the *History of Animals* in a graded scale of perfection, a *scala naturae*, with man at the top. His system had eleven grades of animal, from highest potential to lowest, expressed in their form at birth: the highest gave live birth to hot and wet creatures, the lowest laid cold, dry mineral-like eggs. Animals came above plants, and these in turn were above minerals.[47] He grouped what the modern zoologist would call vertebrates as the hotter "animals with blood", and below them the colder invertebrates as "animals without blood". Those with blood were divided into the live-bearing (mammals), and the egg-laying (birds, reptiles, fish). Those without blood were insects, crustacea (non-shelled – cephalopods, and shelled) and the hard-shelled molluscs (bivalves and gastropods). He recognised that animals did not exactly fit into a linear scale, and noted various exceptions, such as that sharks had a placenta like the tetrapods. To a modern biologist, the explanation, not available to Aristotle, is convergent evolution.[48] He believed that purposive final causes guided all natural processes; this teleological view justified his observed data as an expression of formal design.

Aristotle's *Scala naturae* (highest to lowest)

Group	Examples (given by Aristotle)	Blood	Legs	Souls (Rational, Sensitive, Vegetative)	Qualities (Hot–Cold, Wet–Dry)
Man	Man	with blood	2 legs	R, S, V	Hot, Wet
Live-bearing tetrapods	Cat, hare	with blood	4 legs	S, V	Hot, Wet
Cetaceans	Dolphin, whale	with blood	none	S, V	Hot, Wet
Birds	Bee-eater, nightjar	with blood	2 legs	S, V	Hot, Wet, except Dry eggs
Egg-laying tetrapods	Chameleon, crocodile	with blood	4 legs	S, V	Cold, Wet except scales, eggs
Snakes	Water snake, Ottoman viper	with blood	none	S, V	Cold, Wet except scales, eggs
Egg-laying fishes	Sea bass, parrotfish	with blood	none	S, V	Cold, Wet, including eggs
(Among the egg-laying fishes): placental selachians	Shark, skate	with blood	none	S, V	Cold, Wet, but placenta like tetrapods
Crustaceans	Shrimp, crab	without	many legs	S, V	Cold, Wet except shell

Cephalopods	Squid, octopus	without	tentacles	S, V	Cold, Wet
Hard-shelled animals	Cockle, trumpet snail	without	none	S, V	Cold, Dry (mineral shell)
Larva-bearing insects	Ant, cicada	without	6 legs	S, V	Cold, Dry
Spontaneously-generating	Sponges, worms	without	none	S, V	Cold, Wet or Dry, from earth
Plants	Fig	without	none	V	Cold, Dry
Minerals	Iron	without	none	none	Cold, Dry

Psychology

Soul

Aristotle's psychology, given in his treatise *On the Soul* (*peri psyche*), posits three kinds of soul ("psyches"): the vegetative soul, the sensitive soul, and the rational soul. Humans have a rational soul. The human soul incorporates the powers of the other kinds: Like the vegetative soul it can grow and nourish itself; like the sensitive soul it can experience sensations and move locally. The unique part of the human, rational soul is its ability to receive forms of other things and to compare them using the *nous* (intellect) and *logos* (reason).[49]

For Aristotle, the soul is the form of a living being. Because all beings are composites of form and matter, the form of living beings is that which endows them with what is specific to living beings, e.g. the ability to initiate movement (or in the case of plants, growth and chemical transformations, which Aristotle considers types of movement). In contrast to earlier philosophers, but in accordance with the Egyptians, he placed the rational soul in the heart, rather than the brain. Notable is Aristotle's division of sensation and thought, which generally differed from the concepts of previous philosophers, with the exception of Alcmaeon.

Memory

According to Aristotle in *On the Soul*, memory is the ability to hold a perceived experience in your mind and to distinguish between the internal "appearance" and an occurrence in the past.[50] In other words, a memory is a mental picture (phantasm) that can be recovered. Aristotle believed an impression is left on a semi-fluid bodily organ that undergoes several changes in order to make a memory. A memory occurs when stimuli such as sights or sounds are so complex that the nervous system cannot receive all the impressions at once. These changes are the same as those involved in the operations of sensation, Aristotelian 'common sense', and thinking.[51,52]

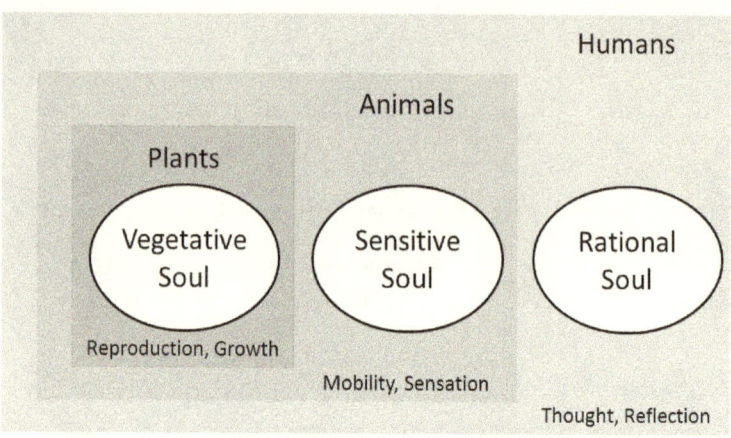

Figure 13: *Aristotle proposed a three-part structure for souls of plants, animals, and humans, making humans unique in having all three types of soul.*

Aristotle uses the term 'memory' for the actual retaining of an experience in the impression that can develop from sensation, and for the intellectual anxiety that comes with the impression because it is formed at a particular time and processing specific contents. Memory is of the past, prediction is of the future, and sensation is of the present. Retrieval of impressions cannot be performed suddenly. A transitional channel is needed and located in our past experiences, both for our previous experience and present experience.[53]

Because Aristotle believes people receive all kinds of sense perceptions and perceive them as impressions, people are continually weaving together new impressions of experiences. To search for these impressions, people search the memory itself.[54] Within the memory, if one experience is offered instead of a specific memory, that person will reject this experience until they find what they are looking for. Recollection occurs when one retrieved experience naturally follows another. If the chain of "images" is needed, one memory will stimulate the next. When people recall experiences, they stimulate certain previous experiences until they reach the one that is needed.[55] Recollection is thus the self-directed activity of retrieving the information stored in a memory impression.[56] Only humans can remember impressions of intellectual activity, such as numbers and words. Animals that have perception of time can retrieve memories of their past observations. Remembering involves only perception of the things remembered and of the time passed.[57]

Aristotle believed the chain of thought, which ends in recollection of certain impressions, was connected systematically in relationships such as similarity,

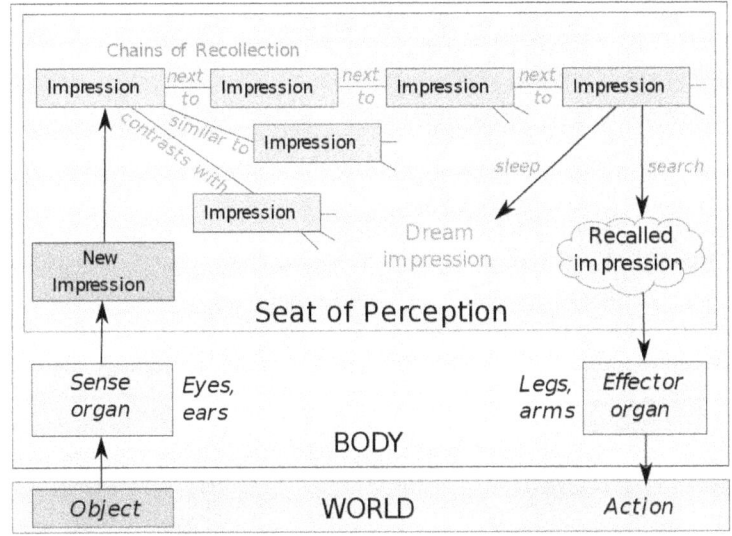

Figure 14: *Senses, perception, memory, dreams, action in Aristotle's psychology. Impressions are stored in the seat of perception, linked by his Laws of Association (similarity, contrast, and contiguity).*

contrast, and contiguity, described in his Laws of Association. Aristotle believed that past experiences are hidden within our mind. A force operates to awaken the hidden material to bring up the actual experience. According to Aristotle, association is the power innate in a mental state, which operates upon the unexpressed remains of former experiences, allowing them to rise and be recalled.[58]

Dreams

Aristotle describes sleep in *On Sleep and Wakefulness*. Sleep takes place as a result of overuse of the senses or of digestion, so it is vital to the body. While a person is asleep, the critical activities, which include thinking, sensing, recalling and remembering, do not function as they do during wakefulness. Since a person cannot sense during sleep they can not have desire, which is the result of sensation. However, the senses are able to work during sleep, albeit differently, unless they are weary.

Dreams do not involve actually sensing a stimulus. In dreams, sensation is still involved, but in an altered manner. Aristotle explains that when a person stares at a moving stimulus such as the waves in a body of water, and then look away, the next thing they look at appears to have a wavelike motion. When a person perceives a stimulus and the stimulus is no longer the focus of their attention, it leaves an impression. When the body is awake and the senses are functioning properly, a person constantly encounters new stimuli to sense and so the impressions of previously perceived stimuli are ignored. However, during sleep the impressions made throughout the day are noticed as there are no new distracting sensory experiences. So, dreams result from these lasting impressions. Since impressions are all that are left and not the exact stimuli, dreams do not resemble the actual waking experience. During sleep, a person is in an altered state of mind. Aristotle compares a sleeping person to a person who is overtaken by strong feelings toward a stimulus. For example, a person who has a strong infatuation with someone may begin to think they see that person everywhere because they are so overtaken by their feelings. Since a person sleeping is in a suggestible state and unable to make judgements, they become easily deceived by what appears in their dreams, like the infatuated person. This leads the person to believe the dream is real, even when the dreams are absurd in nature.

One component of Aristotle's theory of dreams disagrees with previously held beliefs. He claimed that dreams are not foretelling and not sent by a divine being. Aristotle reasoned naturalistically that instances in which dreams do resemble future events are simply coincidences. Aristotle claimed that a dream is first established by the fact that the person is asleep when they experience it. If a person had an image appear for a moment after waking up or if they see something in the dark it is not considered a dream because they were awake when it occurred. Secondly, any sensory experience that is perceived while a person is asleep does not qualify as part of a dream. For example, if, while a person is sleeping, a door shuts and in their dream they hear a door is shut, this sensory experience is not part of the dream. Lastly, the images of dreams must be a result of lasting impressions of waking sensory experiences.

Practical philosophy

Aristotle's practical philosophy covers areas such as ethics, politics, and rhetoric.

Virtues and their accompanying vices

Too little	Virtuous mean	Too much
Humbleness	High-mindedness	Vainglory
Lack of purpose	Right ambition	Over-ambition
Spiritlessness	Good temper	Irascibility

Rudeness	Civility	Obsequiousness
Cowardice	Courage	Rashness
Insensibility	Self-control	Intemperance
Sarcasm	Sincerity	Boastfulness
Boorishness	Wit	Buffoonery
Shamelessness	Modesty	Shyness
Callousness	Just resentment	Spitefulness
Pettiness	Generosity	Vulgarity
Meanness	Liberality	Wastefulness

Ethics

Aristotle considered ethics to be a practical rather than theoretical study, i.e., one aimed at becoming good and doing good rather than knowing for its own sake. He wrote several treatises on ethics, including most notably, the *Nicomachean Ethics*.

Aristotle taught that virtue has to do with the proper function (*ergon*) of a thing. An eye is only a good eye in so much as it can see, because the proper function of an eye is sight. Aristotle reasoned that humans must have a function specific to humans, and that this function must be an activity of the *psuchē* (*soul*) in accordance with reason (*logos*). Aristotle identified such an optimum activity (the virtuous mean, between the accompanying vices of excess or deficiency) of the soul as the aim of all human deliberate action, *eudaimonia*, generally translated as "happiness" or sometimes "well being". To have the potential of ever being happy in this way necessarily requires a good character (*ēthikē aretē*), often translated as moral or ethical virtue or excellence.[59]

Aristotle taught that to achieve a virtuous and potentially happy character requires a first stage of having the fortune to be habituated not deliberately, but by teachers, and experience, leading to a later stage in which one consciously chooses to do the best things. When the best people come to live life this way their practical wisdom (*phronesis*) and their intellect (*nous*) can develop with each other towards the highest possible human virtue, the wisdom of an accomplished theoretical or speculative thinker, or in other words, a philosopher.[60]

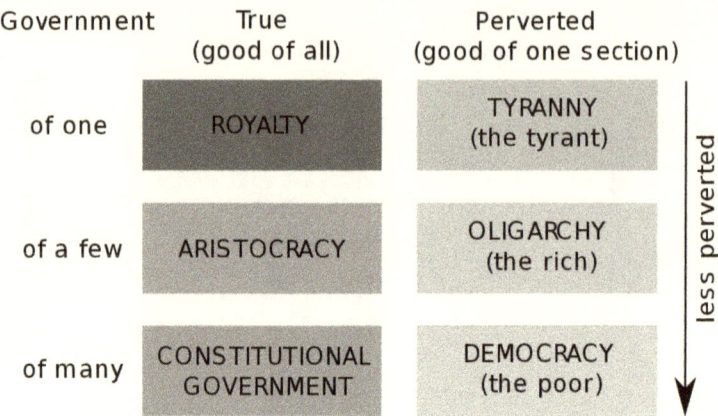

Figure 15: *Aristotle's classifications of political constitutions*

Politics

In addition to his works on ethics, which address the individual, Aristotle addressed the city in his work titled *Politics*. Aristotle considered the city to be a natural community. Moreover, he considered the city to be prior in importance to the family which in turn is prior to the individual, "for the whole must of necessity be prior to the part".[61] He also famously stated that "man is by nature a political animal" and also arguing that humanity's defining factor among others in the animal kingdom is its rationality. Aristotle conceived of politics as being like an organism rather than like a machine, and as a collection of parts none of which can exist without the others. Aristotle's conception of the city is organic, and he is considered one of the first to conceive of the city in this manner.

The common modern understanding of a political community as a modern state is quite different from Aristotle's understanding. Although he was aware of the existence and potential of larger empires, the natural community according to Aristotle was the city (*polis*) which functions as a political "community" or "partnership" (*koinōnia*). The aim of the city is not just to avoid injustice or for economic stability, but rather to allow at least some citizens the possibility to live a good life, and to perform beautiful acts: "The political partnership must be regarded, therefore, as being for the sake of noble actions, not for the sake of living together." This is distinguished from modern approaches, beginning with social contract theory, according to which individuals leave the state of nature because of "fear of violent death" or its "inconveniences."[62]

In *Protrepticus*, the character 'Aristotle' states:

> For we all agree that the most excellent man should rule, i.e., the supreme by nature, and that the law rules and alone is authoritative; but the law is a kind of intelligence, i.e. a discourse based on intelligence. And again, what standard do we have, what criterion of good things, that is more precise than the intelligent man? For all that this man will choose, if the choice is based on his knowledge, are good things and their contraries are bad. And since everybody chooses most of all what conforms to their own proper dispositions (a just man choosing to live justly, a man with bravery to live bravely, likewise a self-controlled man to live with self-control), it is clear that the intelligent man will choose most of all to be intelligent; for this is the function of that capacity. Hence it's evident that, according to the most authoritative judgment, intelligence is supreme among goods.

Economics

Aristotle made substantial contributions to economic thought, especially to thought in the Middle Ages. In *Politics*, Aristotle addresses the city, property, and trade. His response to criticisms of private property, in Lionel Robbins's view, anticipated later proponents of private property among philosophers and economists, as it related to the overall utility of social arrangements. Aristotle believed that although communal arrangements may seem beneficial to society, and that although private property is often blamed for social strife, such evils in fact come from human nature. In *Politics*, Aristotle offers one of the earliest accounts of the origin of money. Money came into use because people became dependent on one another, importing what they needed and exporting the surplus. For the sake of convenience, people then agreed to deal in something that is intrinsically useful and easily applicable, such as iron or silver.

Aristotle's discussions on retail and interest was a major influence on economic thought in the Middle Ages. He had a low opinion of retail, believing that contrary to using money to procure things one needs in managing the household, retail trade seeks to make a profit. It thus uses goods as a means to an end, rather than as an end unto itself. He believed that retail trade was in this way unnatural. Similarly, Aristotle considered making a profit through interest unnatural, as it makes a gain out of the money itself, and not from its use.

Aristotle gave a summary of the function of money that was perhaps remarkably precocious for his time. He wrote that because it is impossible to determine the value of every good through a count of the number of other goods it is worth, the necessity arises of a single universal standard of measurement. Money thus allows for the association of different goods and makes them

Figure 16: *The Blind Oedipus Commending his Children to the Gods (1784) by Bénigne Gagneraux. In his Poetics, Aristotle uses the tragedy Oedipus Tyrannus by Sophocles as an example of how the perfect tragedy should be structured, with a generally good protagonist who starts the play prosperous, but loses everything through some hamartia (fault).*

"commensurable". He goes to on state that money is also useful for future exchange, making it a sort of security. That is, "if we do not want a thing now, we shall be able to get it when we do want it".

Rhetoric and poetics

Aristotle's *Rhetoric* proposes that a speaker can use three basic kinds of appeals to persuade his audience: *ethos* (an appeal to the speaker's character), *pathos* (an appeal to the audience's emotion), and *logos* (an appeal to logical reasoning). He also categorises rhetoric into three genres: epideictic (ceremonial speeches dealing with praise or blame), forensic (judicial speeches over guilt or innocence), and deliberative (speeches calling on an audience to make a decision on an issue). Aristotle also outlines two kinds of rhetorical proofs: *enthymeme* (proof by syllogism) and *paradeigma* (proof by example).

Aristotle writes in his *Poetics* that epic poetry, tragedy, comedy, dithyrambic poetry, painting, sculpture, music, and dance are all fundamentally acts of *mimesis* ("imitation"), each varying in imitation by medium, object, and manner.[63] He applies the term *mimesis* both as a property of a work of art and also as the product of the artist's intention and contends that the audience's realisation of the *mimesis* is vital to understanding the work itself. Aristotle states that *mimesis* is a natural instinct of humanity that separates humans from animals[64] and that all human artistry "follows the pattern of nature". Because of this, Aristotle believed that each of the mimetic arts possesses what Stephen Halliwell calls "highly structured procedures for the achievement of their purposes." For example, music imitates with the media of rhythm and harmony, whereas dance imitates with rhythm alone, and poetry with language. The forms also differ in their object of imitation. Comedy, for instance, is a dramatic imitation of men worse than average; whereas tragedy imitates men slightly better than average. Lastly, the forms differ in their manner of imitation – through narrative or character, through change or no change, and through drama or no drama.[65]

While it is believed that Aristotle's *Poetics* originally comprised two books – one on comedy and one on tragedy – only the portion that focuses on tragedy has survived. Aristotle taught that tragedy is composed of six elements: plot-structure, character, style, thought, spectacle, and lyric poetry.[66] The characters in a tragedy are merely a means of driving the story; and the plot, not the characters, is the chief focus of tragedy. Tragedy is the imitation of action arousing pity and fear, and is meant to effect the catharsis of those same emotions. Aristotle concludes *Poetics* with a discussion on which, if either, is superior: epic or tragic mimesis. He suggests that because tragedy possesses all the attributes of an epic, possibly possesses additional attributes such as spectacle and music, is more unified, and achieves the aim of its mimesis in shorter scope, it can be considered superior to epic.[67] Aristotle was a keen systematic collector of riddles, folklore, and proverbs; he and his school had a special interest in the riddles of the Delphic Oracle and studied the fables of Aesop.

Views on women

Aristotle's analysis of procreation describes an active, ensouling masculine element bringing life to an inert, passive female element. On this ground, proponents of feminist metaphysics have accused Aristotle of misogyny and sexism. However, Aristotle gave equal weight to women's happiness as he did to men's, and commented in his *Rhetoric* that the things that lead to happiness need to be in women as well as men.[68]</ref>

Figure 17: *Frontispiece to a 1644 version of Theophrastus's Historia Plantarum, originally written around 300 BC*

Influence

More than 2300 years after his death, Aristotle remains one of the most influential people who ever lived.[69] He contributed to almost every field of human knowledge then in existence, and he was the founder of many new fields. According to the philosopher Bryan Magee, "it is doubtful whether any human being has ever known as much as he did". Among countless other achievements, Aristotle was the founder of formal logic, pioneered the study of zoology, and left every future scientist and philosopher in his debt through his contributions to the scientific method. Taneli Kukkonen, writing in *The Classical Tradition*, observes that his achievement in founding two sciences is unmatched, and his reach in influencing "every branch of intellectual enterprise" including Western ethical and political theory, theology, rhetoric and literary analysis is equally long. As a result, Kukkonen argues, any analysis of reality today "will almost certainly carry Aristotelian overtones ... evidence of an exceptionally forceful mind." Jonathan Barnes wrote that "an account of Aristotle's intellectual afterlife would be little less than a history of European thought".

On his successor, Theophrastus

Aristotle's pupil and successor, Theophrastus, wrote the *History of Plants*, a pioneering work in botany. Some of his technical terms remain in use, such as carpel from *carpos*, fruit, and pericarp, from *pericarpion*, seed chamber. Theophrastus was much less concerned with formal causes than Aristotle was, instead pragmatically describing how plants functioned.[70]

On later Greek philosophers

The immediate influence of Aristotle's work was felt as the Lyceum grew into the Peripatetic school. Aristotle's notable students included Aristoxenus, Dicaearchus, Demetrius of Phalerum, Eudemos of Rhodes, Harpalus, Hephaestion, Mnason of Phocis, Nicomachus, and Theophrastus. Aristotle's influence over Alexander the Great is seen in the latter's bringing with him on his expedition a host of zoologists, botanists, and researchers. He had also learned a great deal about Persian customs and traditions from his teacher. Although his respect for Aristotle was diminished as his travels made it clear that much of Aristotle's geography was clearly wrong, when the old philosopher released his works to the public, Alexander complained "Thou hast not done well to publish thy acroamatic doctrines; for in what shall I surpass other men if those doctrines wherein I have been trained are to be all men's common property?"[71]

On Hellenistic science

After Theophrastus, the Lyceum failed to produce any original work. Though interest in Aristotle's ideas survived, they were generally taken unquestioningly. It is not until the age of Alexandria under the Ptolemies that advances in biology can be again found.

The first medical teacher at Alexandria, Herophilus of Chalcedon, corrected Aristotle, placing intelligence in the brain, and connected the nervous system to motion and sensation. Herophilus also distinguished between veins and arteries, noting that the latter pulse while the former do not.[72] Though a few ancient atomists such as Lucretius challenged the teleological viewpoint of Aristotelian ideas about life, teleology (and after the rise of Christianity, natural theology) would remain central to biological thought essentially until the 18th and 19th centuries. Ernst Mayr states that there was "nothing of any real consequence in biology after Lucretius and Galen until the Renaissance."

Figure 18: *Islamic portrayal of Aristotle, c. 1220*

On Byzantine scholars

Greek Christian scribes played a crucial role in the preservation of Aristotle by copying all the extant Greek language manuscripts of the corpus. The first Greek Christians to comment extensively on Aristotle were Philoponus, Elias, and David in the sixth century, and Stephen of Alexandria in the early seventh century.[73] Philoponus stands out for having attempted a fundamental critique of Aristotle's views on the eternity of the world, movement, and other elements of Aristotelian thought.[74] After a hiatus of several centuries, formal commentary by Eustratius and Michael of Ephesus reappears in the late eleventh and early twelfth centuries, apparently sponsored by Anna Comnena.[75]

On the medieval Islamic world

Aristotle was one of the most revered Western thinkers in early Islamic theology. Most of the still extant works of Aristotle, as well as a number of the original Greek commentaries, were translated into Arabic and studied by Muslim philosophers, scientists and scholars. Averroes, Avicenna and Alpharabius, who wrote on Aristotle in great depth, also influenced Thomas Aquinas and other Western Christian scholastic philosophers. Alkindus considered Aristotle the outstanding and unique representative of philosophy[76] and Averroes spoke of Aristotle as the "exemplar" for all future philosophers.[77] Medieval

Figure 19: *Woodcut of Aristotle ridden by Phyllis by Hans Baldung, 1515*

Muslim scholars regularly described Aristotle as the "First Teacher". The title "teacher" was first given to Aristotle by Muslim scholars, and was later used by Western philosophers (as in the famous poem of Dante) who were influenced by the tradition of Islamic philosophy.

In accordance with the Greek theorists, the Muslims considered Aristotle to be a dogmatic philosopher, the author of a closed system, and believed that Aristotle shared with Plato essential tenets of thought. Some went so far as to credit Aristotle himself with neo-Platonic metaphysical ideas.[78]

On medieval Europe

With the loss of the study of ancient Greek in the early medieval Latin West, Aristotle was practically unknown there from c. AD 600 to c. 1100 except through the Latin translation of the *Organon* made by Boethius. In the twelfth and thirteenth centuries, interest in Aristotle revived and Latin Christians had translations made, both from Arabic translations, such as those by Gerard of Cremona, and from the original Greek, such as those by James of Venice and William of Moerbeke. After the Scholastic Thomas Aquinas wrote his *Summa Theologica*, working from Moerbeke's translations and calling Aristotle "The Philosopher",[79] the demand for Aristotle's writings grew, and the

Greek manuscripts returned to the West, stimulating a revival of Aristotelianism in Europe that continued into the Renaissance. These thinkers blended Aristotelian philosophy with Christianity, bringing the thought of Ancient Greece into the Middle Ages. Scholars such as Boethius, Peter Abelard, and John Buridan worked on Aristotelian logic.

The medieval English poet Chaucer describes his student as being happy by having

> *at his beddes heed*
>
> *Twenty bookes, clad in blak or reed,*
>
> *Of aristotle and his philosophie,*

A cautionary medieval tale held that Aristotle advised his pupil Alexander to avoid the king's seductive mistress, Phyllis, but was himself captivated by her, and allowed her to ride him. Phyllis had secretly told Alexander what to expect, and he witnessed Phyllis proving that a woman's charms could overcome even the greatest philosopher's male intellect. Artists such as Hans Baldung produced a series of illustrations of the popular theme.

The Italian poet Dante says of Aristotle in *The Divine Comedy*:

Dante *L'Inferno*, Canto IV. 131–135	Translation *Hell*
vidi 'l maestro di color che sanno seder tra filosofica famiglia. Tutti lo miran, tutti onor li fanno: quivi vid'ïo Socrate e Platone che 'nnanzi a li altri più presso li stanno;	I saw the Master there of those who know, Amid the philosophic family, By all admired, and by all reverenced; There Plato too I saw, and Socrates, Who stood beside him closer than the rest.

On Early Modern scientists

In the Early Modern period, scientists such as William Harvey in England and Galileo Galilei in Italy reacted against the theories of Aristotle and other classical era thinkers like Galen, establishing new theories based to some degree on observation and experiment. Harvey demonstrated the circulation of the blood, establishing that the heart functioned as a pump rather than being the seat of the soul and the controller of the body's heat, as Aristotle thought. Galileo used more doubtful arguments to displace Aristotle's physics, proposing that bodies all fall at the same speed whatever their weight.

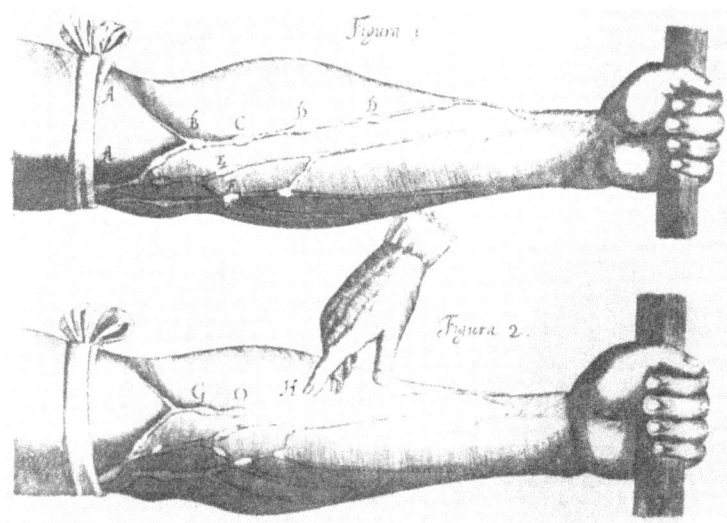

Figure 20: *William Harvey's Exercitatio Anatomica de Motu Cordis et Sanguinis in Animalibus, 1628, showed that the blood circulated, contrary to classical era thinking.*

On 19th-century thinkers

The 19th-century German philosopher Friedrich Nietzsche has been said to have taken nearly all of his political philosophy from Aristotle.[80] Aristotle rigidly separated action from production, and argued for the deserved subservience of some people ("natural slaves"), and the natural superiority (virtue, *arete*) of others. It was Martin Heidegger, not Nietzsche, who elaborated a new interpretation of Aristotle, intended to warrant his deconstruction of scholastic and philosophical tradition.

The English mathematician George Boole fully accepted Aristotle's logic, but decided "to go under, over, and beyond" it with his system of algebraic logic in his 1854 book *The Laws of Thought*. This gives logic a mathematical foundation with equations, enables it to solve equations as well as check validity, and allows it to handle a wider class of problems by expanding propositions of any number of terms, not just two.[81]

Figure 21: *"That most enduring of romantic images, Aristotle tutoring the future conqueror Alexander". Illustration by Charles Laplante, 1866*

Modern rejection and rehabilitation

During the 20th century, Aristotle's work was widely criticised. The philosopher Bertrand Russell argued that "almost every serious intellectual advance has had to begin with an attack on some Aristotelian doctrine". Russell called Aristotle's ethics "repulsive", and labelled his logic "as definitely antiquated as Ptolemaic astronomy". Russell stated that these errors made it difficult to do historical justice to Aristotle, until one remembered what an advance he made upon all of his predecessors. In 1985, the biologist Peter Medawar could still state in "pure seventeenth century"[7] tones that Aristotle had assembled "a strange and generally speaking rather tiresome farrago of hearsay, imperfect observation, wishful thinking and credulity amounting to downright gullibility".[7]

By the start of the 21st century, however, Aristotle was taken more seriously: Kukkonen noted that "In the best 20th-century scholarship Aristotle comes alive as a thinker wrestling with the full weight of the Greek philosophical tradition." Ayn Rand accredited Aristotle as "the greatest philosopher in history" and cited him as a major influence on her thinking. More recently, Alasdair MacIntyre has attempted to reform what he calls the Aristotelian tradition in a way that is anti-elitist and capable of disputing the claims of both liberals and

Figure 22: *First page of a 1566 edition of the Nicomachean Ethics in Greek and Latin*

Nietzscheans. Kukkonen observed, too, that "that most enduring of romantic images, Aristotle tutoring the future conqueror Alexander" remained current, as in the 2004 film *Alexander*, while the "firm rules" of Aristotle's theory of drama have ensured a role for the *Poetics* in Hollywood.

Biologists continue to be interested in Aristotle's thinking. Armand Marie Leroi has reconstructed Aristotle's biology,[82] while Niko Tinbergen's four questions, based on Aristotle's four causes, are used to analyse animal behaviour; they examine function, phylogeny, mechanism, and ontogeny.[83]

Surviving works

Corpus Aristotelicum

The works of Aristotle that have survived from antiquity through medieval manuscript transmission are collected in the Corpus Aristotelicum. These texts, as opposed to Aristotle's lost works, are technical philosophical treatises from within Aristotle's school. Reference to them is made according to the organisation of Immanuel Bekker's Royal Prussian Academy edition (*Aristotelis Opera edidit Academia Regia Borussica*, Berlin, 1831–1870), which in turn is based on ancient classifications of these works.[84]

Loss and preservation

Aristotle wrote his works on papyrus scrolls, the common writing medium of that era.[85]</ref> His writings are divisible into two groups: the "exoteric", intended for the public, and the "esoteric", for use within the Lyceum school.[86] Aristotle's "lost" works stray considerably in characterisation from the surviving Aristotelian corpus. Whereas the lost works appear to have been originally written with a view to subsequent publication, the surviving works mostly resemble lecture notes not intended for publication.[87,88] Cicero's description of Aristotle's literary style as "a river of gold" must have applied to the published works, not the surviving notes.[89]</ref> A major question in the history of Aristotle's works is how the exoteric writings were all lost, and how the ones we now possess came to us. The consensus is that Andronicus of Rhodes collected the esoteric works of Aristotle's school which existed in the form of smaller, separate works, distinguished them from those of Theophrastus and other Peripatetics, edited them, and finally compiled them into the more cohesive, larger works as they are known today.[90]

Legacy

Depictions

Aristotle has been depicted by major artists including Lucas Cranach the Elder, Justus van Gent, Raphael, Paolo Veronese, Jusepe de Ribera, Rembrandt, and Francesco Hayez over the centuries. Among the best-known is Raphael's fresco *The School of Athens*, in the Vatican's Apostolic Palace, where the figures of Plato and Aristotle are central to the image, at the architectural vanishing point, reflecting their importance. Rembrandt's *Aristotle with a Bust of Homer*, too, is a celebrated work, showing the knowing philosopher and the blind Homer from an earlier age: as the art critic Jonathan Jones writes, "this painting will remain one of the greatest and most mysterious in the world, ensnaring us in its musty, glowing, pitch-black, terrible knowledge of time."

Figure 23: *Nuremberg Chronicle anachronistically shows Aristotle in a medieval scholar's clothing. Ink and watercolour on paper, 1493*

Figure 24: *Aristotle by Justus van Gent. Oil on panel, c. 1476*

Figure 25: *Phyllis and Aristotle by Lucas Cranach the Elder. Oil on panel, 1530*

Figure 26: *Aristotle by Paolo Veronese, Biblioteka Marciana. Oil on canvas, 1560s*

Figure 27: *Aristotle and Campaspe, Alessandro Turchi (attrib.) Oil on canvas, 1713*

Figure 28: *Aristotle by Jusepe de Ribera. Oil on canvas, 1637*

Figure 29: *Aristotle with a Bust of Homer by Rembrandt. Oil on canvas, 1653*

Figure 30: *Aristotle by Johann Jakob Dorner the Elder. Oil on canvas, by 1813*

Figure 31: *Aristotle by Francesco Hayez. Oil on canvas, 1811*

Eponyms

The Aristotle Mountains in Antarctica are named after Aristotle. He was the first person known to conjecture, in his book *Meteorology*, the existence of a landmass in the southern high-latitude region and called it *Antarctica*. Aristoteles is a crater on the Moon bearing the classical form of Aristotle's name.

References

Sources

- Barnes, Jonathan (1995). "Life and Work"[91]. *The Cambridge Companion to Aristotle*. Cambridge University Press. ISBN 978-0-521-42294-9.<templatestyles src="Module:Citation/CS1/styles.css"></templatestyles>
- Bloch, David (2007). *Aristotle on Memory and Recollection*[92]. ISBN 978-90-04-16046-0.<templatestyles src="Module:Citation/CS1/styles.css"></templatestyles>
- Carruthers, Mary (2007). *The Book of Memory: A Study of Memory in Medieval Culture*[93]. ISBN 978-0-521-42973-3.<templatestyles src="Module:Citation/CS1/styles.css"></templatestyles>

- Leroi, Armand Marie (2015). *The Lagoon: How Aristotle Invented Science*. Bloomsbury. ISBN 978-1408836224.<templatestyles src="Module:Citation/CS1/styles.css"></templatestyles>
- Lloyd, G. E. R. (1968). *The critic of Plato. Aristotle: The Growth and Structure of His Thought*. Cambridge University Press. ISBN 978-0-521-09456-6.<templatestyles src="Module:Citation/CS1/styles.css"></templatestyles>
- Sorabji, Richard (1990). *Aristotle Transformed*. Duckworth. ISBN 978-0715622544.<templatestyles src="Module:Citation/CS1/styles.css"></templatestyles>
- Taylor, Henry Osborn (1922). "Chapter 3: Aristotle's Biology". *Greek Biology and Medicine*[94]. Archived from the original[95] on 27 March 2006. Retrieved 3 January 2017.<templatestyles src="Module:Citation/CS1/styles.css"></templatestyles>
- Warren, Howard (1921). *A History of the Association Psychology*[96]. OCLC 21010604[97].<templatestyles src="Module:Citation/CS1/styles.css"></templatestyles>

Further reading

The secondary literature on Aristotle is vast. The following references are only a small selection. <templatestyles src="Template:Refbegin/styles.css" />

- Ackrill J. L. (1997). *Essays on Plato and Aristotle*, Oxford University Press.
- Ackrill, J. L. (1981). *Aristotle the Philosopher*. Oxford University Press.<templatestyles src="Module:Citation/CS1/styles.css"></templatestyles>
- Adler, Mortimer J. (1978). *Aristotle for Everybody*. Macmillan.<templatestyles src="Module:Citation/CS1/styles.css"></templatestyles>
- Ammonius (1991). Cohen, S. Marc; Matthews, Gareth B, eds. *On Aristotle's Categories*. Cornell University Press. ISBN 978-0-8014-2688-9.<templatestyles src="Module:Citation/CS1/styles.css"></templatestyles>
- Aristotle (1908–1952). *The Works of Aristotle Translated into English Under the Editorship of W. D. Ross, 12 vols*. Clarendon Press.<templatestyles src="Module:Citation/CS1/styles.css"></templatestyles> These translations are available in several places online; see External links.
- Bakalis, Nikolaos. (2005). *Handbook of Greek Philosophy: From Thales to the Stoics Analysis and Fragments*, Trafford Publishing <templatestyles src="Module:Citation/CS1/styles.css" />ISBN 978-1-4120-4843-9

- Bocheński, I. M. (1951). *Ancient Formal Logic*. North-Holland.<templatestyles src="Module:Citation/CS1/styles.css"></templatestyles>
- Bolotin, David (1998). *An Approach to Aristotle's Physics: With Particular Attention to the Role of His Manner of Writing*. Albany: SUNY Press. A contribution to our understanding of how to read Aristotle's scientific works.
- Burnyeat, M. F. *et al.* (1979). *Notes on Book Zeta of Aristotle's Metaphysics*. Oxford: Sub-faculty of Philosophy.
- Cantor, Norman F.; Klein, Peter L., eds. (1969). *Ancient Thought: Plato and Aristotle*. Monuments of Western Thought. **1**. Blaisdell.<templatestyles src="Module:Citation/CS1/styles.css"></templatestyles>
- Chappell, V. (1973). "Aristotle's Conception of Matter". *Journal of Philosophy*. **70** (19): 679–96. doi:10.2307/2025076[98]. JSTOR 2025076[99].<templatestyles src="Module:Citation/CS1/styles.css"></templatestyles>
- Code, Alan (1995). Potentiality in Aristotle's Science and Metaphysics, Pacific Philosophical Quarterly 76.
- Ferguson, John (1972). *Aristotle*. Twayne Publishers.<templatestyles src="Module:Citation/CS1/styles.css"></templatestyles>
- De Groot, Jean (2014). *Aristotle's Empiricism: Experience and Mechanics in the 4th Century BC*, Parmenides Publishing, <templatestyles src="Module:Citation/CS1/styles.css" />ISBN 978-1-930972-83-4
- Frede, Michael (1987). *Essays in Ancient Philosophy*. Minneapolis: University of Minnesota Press.
- Fuller, B.A.G. (1923). *Aristotle*. History of Greek Philosophy. **3**. Cape.<templatestyles src="Module:Citation/CS1/styles.css"></templatestyles>
- Gendlin, Eugene T. (2012). *Line by Line Commentary on Aristotle's De Anima*[100], Volume 1: Books I & II; Volume 2: Book III. The Focusing Institute.
- Gill, Mary Louise (1989). *Aristotle on Substance: The Paradox of Unity*. Princeton University Press.
- Guthrie, W. K. C. (1981). *A History of Greek Philosophy*. **6**. Cambridge University Press.<templatestyles src="Module:Citation/CS1/styles.css"></templatestyles>
- Halper, Edward C. (2009). *One and Many in Aristotle's Metaphysics, Volume 1: Books Alpha – Delta*, Parmenides Publishing, <templatestyles src="Module:Citation/CS1/styles.css" />ISBN 978-1-930972-21-6.
- Halper, Edward C. (2005). *One and Many in Aristotle's Metaphysics, Volume 2: The Central Books*, Parmenides Publishing, <templatestyles src="Module:Citation/CS1/styles.css" />ISBN 978-1-930972-05-6.

- Irwin, T. H. (1988). *Aristotle's First Principles*[101]. Oxford: Clarendon Press, <templatestyles src="Module:Citation/CS1/styles.css" />ISBN 0-19-824290-5.
- Jaeger, Werner (1948). Robinson, Richard, ed. *Aristotle: Fundamentals of the History of His Development* (2nd ed.). Clarendon Press.<templatestyles src="Module:Citation/CS1/styles.css"></templatestyles>
- Jori, Alberto (2003). *Aristotele*, Bruno Mondadori (Prize 2003 of the "International Academy of the History of Science") <templatestyles src="Module:Citation/CS1/styles.css" />ISBN 978-88-424-9737-0.
- Kiernan, Thomas P., ed. (1962). *Aristotle Dictionary*. Philosophical Library.<templatestyles src="Module:Citation/CS1/styles.css"></templatestyles>
- Knight, Kelvin (2007). *Aristotelian Philosophy: Ethics and Politics from Aristotle to MacIntyre*, Polity Press.
- Lewis, Frank A. (1991). *Substance and Predication in Aristotle*. Cambridge University Press.
- Lord, Carnes (1984). *Introduction to* The Politics, *by Aristotle*. Chicago University Press.
- Loux, Michael J. (1991). Primary Ousia: An Essay on Aristotle's Metaphysics Z and H. Ithaca, NY: Cornell University Press.
- Maso, Stefano (Ed.), Natali, Carlo (Ed.), Seel, Gerhard (Ed.) (2012) *Reading Aristotle: Physics VII.3: What is Alteration? Proceedings of the International ESAP-HYELE Conference*, Parmenides Publishing. <templatestyles src="Module:Citation/CS1/styles.css" />ISBN 978-1-930972-73-5
- McKeon, Richard (1973). *Introduction to Aristotle* (2nd ed.). University of Chicago Press.<templatestyles src="Module:Citation/CS1/styles.css"></templatestyles>
- Owen, G. E. L. (1965c). "The Platonism of Aristotle". *Proceedings of the British Academy*. **50**: 125–150.<templatestyles src="Module:Citation/CS1/styles.css"></templatestyles> [Reprinted in J. Barnes, M. Schofield, and R. R. K. Sorabji, eds.(1975). *Articles on Aristotle* Vol 1. Science. London: Duckworth 14–34.]
- Pangle, Lorraine Smith (2003). *Aristotle and the Philosophy of Friendship*. Cambridge University Press.
- Plato (1979). Allen, Harold Joseph; Wilbur, James B, eds. *The Worlds of Plato and Aristotle*. Prometheus Books.<templatestyles src="Module:Citation/CS1/styles.css"></templatestyles>
- Reeve, C. D. C. (2000). *Substantial Knowledge: Aristotle's Metaphysics*. Hackett.

- Rose, Lynn E. (1968). *Aristotle's Syllogistic*. Charles C Thomas.
- Ross, Sir David (1995). *Aristotle* (6th ed.). Routledge.
- Scaltsas, T. (1994). *Substances and Universals in Aristotle's Metaphysics*. Cornell University Press.
- Strauss, Leo (1964). "On Aristotle's *Politics*", in *The City and Man*, Rand McNally.
- Swanson, Judith (1992). *The Public and the Private in Aristotle's Political Philosophy*. Cornell University Press.
- Veatch, Henry B. (1974). *Aristotle: A Contemporary Appreciation*. Indiana University Press.
- Woods, M. J. (1991b). "Universals and Particular Forms in Aristotle's Metaphysics". *Aristotle and the Later Tradition*. Oxford Studies in Ancient Philosophy. Suppl. pp. 41–56.

External links

 Greek Wikisourcehas original text related to this article: Ἀριστοτέλης

Library resources about
Aristotle

- Online books[102]
- Resources in your library[103]
- Resources in other libraries[104]

By Aristotle

- Online books[105]
- Resources in your library[106]
- Resources in other libraries[107]

- Aristotle[108] at *Encyclopædia Britannica*
- Aristotle[109] at PhilPapers
- Aristotle[110] at the Indiana Philosophy Ontology Project
- At the Internet Encyclopedia of Philosophy:
  - Aristotle (general article)[111]
  - Biology[112]
  - Ethics[113]

- Logic[114]
- Metaphysics[115]
- Motion and its Place in Nature[116]
- Poetics[117]
- Politics[118]
- From the Stanford Encyclopedia of Philosophy:
  - Aristotle (general article)[119]
  - Aristotle in the Renaissance[120]
  - Biology[121]
  - Causality[122]
  - Commentators on Aristotle[123]
  - Ethics[124]
  - Logic[125]
  - Mathematics[126]
  - Metaphysics[127]
  - Natural philosophy[128]
  - Non-contradiction[129]
  - Political theory[130]
  - Psychology[131]
  - Rhetoric[132]
- 🕮 Turner, William (1907). "Aristotle". *Catholic Encyclopedia*. **1**.<templatestyles src="Module:Citation/CS1/styles.css"></templatestyles>
- 🕮 Laërtius, Diogenes (1925). "The Peripatetics: Aristotle". *Lives of the Eminent Philosophers*. **1:5**. Translated by Hicks, Robert Drew (Two volume ed.). Loeb Classical Library.<templatestyles src="Module:Citation/CS1/styles.css"></templatestyles>

Collections of works

- At Massachusetts Institute of Technology[133]
- Works by Aristotle[134] at Project Gutenberg
- Works by or about Aristotle[135] at Internet Archive
- Works by Aristotle[136] at LibriVox (public domain audiobooks) 🔊
- Works by Aristotle[137] at Open Library
- (in English) (in Greek) Perseus Project[138] at Tufts University
- At the University of Adelaide[139]
- (in Greek) (in French) P. Remacle[140]
- The 11-volume 1837 Bekker edition of *Aristotle's Works* in Greek (PDF[141] · DJVU[142])
- Bekker's Prussian Academy of Sciences edition of the complete works: vol. 1[143] - vol. 2[144] - vol. 3[145] - vol. 4[146] - vol. 5[147]

Appendix

References

[1] Aristotle (350 B.C.). *On the soul* http://classics.mit.edu/Aristotle/soul.html. Translated by J. A. Smith

[2] "Aristotle" http://www.collinsdictionary.com/dictionary/english/aristotle entry in *Collins English Dictionary*.

[3] That these dates (the first half of the Olympiad year 384/383 BC, and in 322 shortly before the death of Demosthenes) are correct was shown by August Boeckh (*Kleine Schriften* VI 195); for further discussion, see Felix Jacoby on *FGrHist* 244 F 38. Ingemar Düring, *Aristotle in the Ancient Biographical Tradition*, Göteborg, 1957, p. 253

[4] Russell, Bertrand. *A History of Western Philosophy*, Simon & Schuster, 1972. Book One. Ancient Philosophy, Part II. Socrates, Plato and Aristotle, Chapter XXII.

[5] Barnes 1995, p. 16.

[6] Barnes 1995, p. 9.

[7] Leroi 2015, p. 353.

[8] See Shields, C., "Aristotle's Philosophical Life and Writings" in *The Oxford Handbook of Aristotle* (Oxford University Press, 2012), , . Düring, I., *Aristotle in the Ancient Biographical Tradition* (Göteborg, 1957) covers ancient biographies of Aristotle.

[9] William George Smith, *Dictionary of Greek and Roman Biography and Mythology*, , http://www.ancientlibrary.com/smith-bio/2421.html

[10] *Vita Marciana* 41, cf. Aelian *Varia historica* 3.36, Ingemar Düring, *Aristotle in the Ancient Biographical Tradition*, Göteborg, 1957, T44a-e.

[11] This type of syllogism, with all three terms in 'a', is known by the traditional (medieval) mnemonic **Barbara**. UNIQ-ref-0-f62a4c862e50a52a-QINU

[12] M is the Middle (here, Men), S is the Subject (Greeks), P is the Predicate (mortal). UNIQ-ref-1-f62a4c862e50a52a-QINU

[13] The first equation can be read as 'It is not true that there exists an x such that x is a man and that x is not mortal.'<ref>

[14] "Prior Analytics", 24b18–20; Stanford Encyclopedia of Philosophy: *Ancient Logic*: Aristotle: Non-Modal Syllogistic http://plato.stanford.edu/entries/logic-ancient/#SynSemSen and *Ancient Logic*: Aristotle: Modal Logic http://plato.stanford.edu/entries/logic-ancient/#ModLog

[15] Aristotle, *Metaphysics* VIII 1043a 10–30

[16] Aristotle, *Metaphysics* IX 1050a 5–10

[17] Aristotle, *Metaphysics* VIII 1045a–b

[18] Lloyd 1968, pp. 43–47.

[19] Lloyd 1968, pp. 133–139, 166–169.

[20] Rhett Allain notes that Newton's First Law is "essentially a direct reply to Aristotle, that the natural state is *not to change* motion. UNIQ-ref-2-f62a4c862e50a52a-QINU

[21] Leonard Susskind comments that Aristotle had clearly never gone ice skating or he would have seen that it takes force to stop an object.

[22] For heavenly bodies like the Sun, Moon, and stars, the observed motions are "to a very good approximation" circular around the Earth's centre, (for example, the apparent rotation of the sky because of the rotation of the Earth, and the rotation of the moon around the Earth) as Aristotle stated.<ref name="Rovelli2015">

[23] Drabkin quotes numerous passages from *Physics* and *On the Heavens* (*De Caelo*) which state Aristotle's laws of motion.Aristotle (350 B.C.). *On the soul* http://classics.mit.edu/Aristotle/soul.html. Translated by J. A. Smith

[24] Drabkin agrees that density is treated quantitatively in this passage, but without a sharp definition of density as weight per unit volume. "Aristotle" http://www.collinsdictionary.com/dictionary/english/aristotle entry in *Collins English Dictionary*.

[25] Philoponus and Galileo correctly objected that for the transient phase (still increasing in speed) with heavy objects falling a short distance, the law does not apply: Galileo used balls on a

short incline to show this. Rovelli notes that "Two heavy balls with the same shape and different weight do fall at different speeds from an aeroplane, confirming Aristotle's theory, not Galileo's."That these dates (the first half of the Olympiad year 384/383 BC, and in 322 shortly before the death of Demosthenes) are correct was shown by August Boeckh (*Kleine Schriften* VI 195); for further discussion, see Felix Jacoby on *FGrHist* 244 F 38. Ingemar Düring, *Aristotle in the Ancient Biographical Tradition*, Göteborg, 1957, p. 253

[26] Leroi 2015, pp. 88–90.
[27] Leroi 2015, pp. 91–92, 369–373.
[28] Aristotle, *Physics* 2.6
[29] Aristotle, *Meteorology* 1.8, trans. E.W. Webster, rev. J. Barnes.
[30] Aristotle. *Meteorology*. Book 1, Part 14
[31] Leroi 2015, p. 7.
[32] Leroi 2015, p. 14.
[33] Leroi 2015, pp. 196, 248.
[34] Leroi 2015, pp. 66–74, 137.
[35] Leroi 2015, pp. 118–119.
[36] Leroi 2015, p. 73.
[37] Leroi 2015, pp. 135–136.
[38] Leroi 2015, p. 206.
[39] Leroi 2015, p. 273.
[40] Taylor 1922, p. 42.
[41] Leroi 2015, pp. 361–365.
[42] Leroi 2015, pp. 197–200.
[43] Leroi 2015, pp. 365–368.
[44] Taylor 1922, p. 49.
[45] Leroi 2015, p. 408.
[46] Leroi 2015, pp. 72–74.
[47] see also:
[48] Leroi 2015, pp. 111–119.
[49] Leroi 2015, pp. 156–163.
[50] Bloch 2007, p. 12.
[51] Bloch 2007, p. 61.
[52] Carruthers 2007, p. 16.
[53] Bloch 2007, p. 25.
[54] Warren 1921, p. 30.
[55] Warren 1921, p. 25.
[56] Carruthers 2007, p. 19.
[57] Warren 1921, p. 296.
[58] Warren 1921, p. 259.
[59] Nicomachean Ethics Book I. See for example chapter 7 1098a http://www.perseus.tufts.edu/hopper/text?doc=Perseus%3Atext%3A1999.01.0054%3Abekker%20page%3D1098a.
[60] Nicomachean Ethics Book VI.
[61] Politics 1253a19–24
[62] For a different reading of social and economic processes in the *Nicomachean Ethics* and *Politics* see Polanyi, Karl (1957) "Aristotle Discovers the Economy" in *Primitive, Archaic and Modern Economies: Essays of Karl Polanyi* ed. G. Dalton, Boston 1971, 78–115
[63] Aristotle, *Poetics* I 1447a
[64] Aristotle, *Poetics* IV
[65] Aristotle, *Poetics* III
[66] Aristotle, *Poetics* VI
[67] Aristotle, *Poetics* XXVI
[68] "Where, as among the Lacedaemonians, the state of women is bad, almost half of human life is spoilt."<ref>
[69] Leroi 2015, p. 8.
[70] Mayr, *The Growth of Biological Thought*, pp. 90–91; Mason, *A History of the Sciences*, p. 46

[71] Plutarch, of Alexander http://penelope.uchicago.edu/Thayer/e/roman/texts/plutarch/lives/alexander*/3.html"Life, Part 1, 7:7. From Loeb Classical Library, Vol VII, 1919.
[72] Mason, *A History of the Sciences* p. 56
[73] Sorabji 1990, pp. 20, 28, 35–36.
[74] Sorabji 1990, pp. 233–274.
[75] Sorabji 1990, pp. 20–21; 28–29, 393–406; 407–408.
[76] *Rasa'il* I, 103, 17, Abu Rida
[77] *Comm. Magnum* in Aristotle, *De Anima*, III, 2, 43 Crawford
[78] *Encyclopedia of Islam, Aristutalis*
[79] E.g. *Summa Theologica*, Part I, Question 3
[80] Durant, p. 86
[81] Boole, George (2003) [1854]. *The Laws of Thought*, facsimile, with introduction by J. Corcoran. Buffalo: Prometheus Books (2003). Reviewed by James van Evra in *Philosophy in Review* **24** (2004). pp. 167–169.
[82] Leroi 2015.
[83] Hladký, V. & Havlíček, J. (2013). Was Tinbergen an Aristotelian? Comparison of Tinbergen's Four Whys and Aristotle's Four Causes http://ishe.org/wp-content/uploads/2015/04/HEB_2013_28_4_3-11.pdf. *Human Ethology Bulletin*, 28(4), 3-11
[84] Bekker, Immanuel (editor). (1831–1870) *Aristotelis Opera edidit Academia Regia Borussica* https://archive.org/details/bub_gb_jMz9zVYu9Q0C, Berlin. (5 volumes).
[85] "When the Roman dictator Sulla invaded Athens in 86 BC, he brought back to Rome a fantastic prize – Aristotle's library. Books then were papyrus rolls, from 10 to 20 feet long, and since Aristotle's death in 322 BC, worms and damp had done their worst. The rolls needed repairing, and the texts clarifying and copying on to new papyrus (imported from Egypt – Moses' bulrushes). The man in Rome who put Aristotle's library in order was a Greek scholar, Tyrannio."<ref name="Telegraph19May2001">
[86] Aristotle: *Nicomachean Ethics* 1102a26–27. Aristotle himself never uses the term "esoteric" or "acroamatic". For other passages where Aristotle speaks of *exōterikoi logoi*, see W. D. Ross, *Aristotle's Metaphysics* (1953), vol. 2, pp. 408–10. Ross defends an interpretation according to which the phrase, at least in Aristotle's own works, usually refers generally to "discussions not peculiar to the Peripatetic school", rather than to specific works of Aristotle's own.
[87] Irwin, Terence; Fine, Gail, Cornell University, *Aristotle: Introductory Readings*. Indianapolis, Indiana: Hackett Publishing Company, (1996), Introduction, pp. xi–xii.
[88] Barnes 1995, p. 12.
[89] "*veniet flumen orationis aureum fundens Aristoteles*", (Google translation: "Aristotle will come pouring forth a golden stream of eloquence").<ref>
[90] Barnes 1995, pp. 10–15.
[91] https://books.google.com/books?id=WBqQOqM5dfsC
[92] https//books.google.com
[93] https//books.google.com
[94] https://web.archive.org/web/20060327222953/http://www.ancientlibrary.com/medicine/0051.html
[95] http://www.ancientlibrary.com/medicine/0051.html
[96] https//books.google.com
[97] //www.worldcat.org/oclc/21010604
[98] //doi.org/10.2307%2F2025076
[99] //www.jstor.org/stable/2025076
[100] http://www.focusing.org/aristotle/
[101] http://www.cyjack.com/cognition/Aristotle%27s%20first%20principles.pdf
[102] //tools.wmflabs.org/ftl/cgi-bin/ftl?st=wp&su=Aristotle&library=OLBP
[103] //tools.wmflabs.org/ftl/cgi-bin/ftl?st=wp&su=Aristotle
[104] //tools.wmflabs.org/ftl/cgi-bin/ftl?st=wp&su=Aristotle&library=0CHOOSE0
[105] //tools.wmflabs.org/ftl/cgi-bin/ftl?at=wp&au=Aristotle&library=OLBP
[106] //tools.wmflabs.org/ftl/cgi-bin/ftl?at=wp&au=Aristotle
[107] //tools.wmflabs.org/ftl/cgi-bin/ftl?at=wp&au=Aristotle&library=0CHOOSE0
[108] https://www.britannica.com/EBchecked/topic/34560

[109] https://philpapers.org/browse/aristotle
[110] https://inpho.cogs.indiana.edu/thinker/2553
[111] http://www.iep.utm.edu/aristotl/
[112] http://www.iep.utm.edu/aris-bio/
[113] http://www.iep.utm.edu/aris-eth/
[114] http://www.iep.utm.edu/aris-log/
[115] http://www.iep.utm.edu/aris-met/
[116] http://www.iep.utm.edu/aris-mot/
[117] http://www.iep.utm.edu/aris-poe/
[118] http://www.iep.utm.edu/aris-pol/
[119] http://plato.stanford.edu/entries/aristotle
[120] http://plato.stanford.edu/entries/aristotelianism-renaissance/
[121] http://plato.stanford.edu/entries/aristotle-biology/
[122] http://plato.stanford.edu/entries/aristotle-causality/
[123] http://plato.stanford.edu/entries/aristotle-commentators/
[124] http://plato.stanford.edu/entries/aristotle-ethics/
[125] http://plato.stanford.edu/entries/aristotle-logic/
[126] http://plato.stanford.edu/entries/aristotle-mathematics/
[127] http://plato.stanford.edu/entries/aristotle-metaphysics/
[128] http://plato.stanford.edu/entries/aristotle-natphil/
[129] http://plato.stanford.edu/entries/aristotle-noncontradiction/
[130] http://plato.stanford.edu/entries/aristotle-politics/
[131] http://plato.stanford.edu/entries/aristotle-psychology/
[132] http://plato.stanford.edu/entries/aristotle-rhetoric/
[133] http://classics.mit.edu/Browse/index-Aristotle.html
[134] https://www.gutenberg.org/author/Aristotle
[135] https//archive.org
[136] https://librivox.org/author/602
[137] //openlibrary.org/authors/OL22105A
[138] http://www.perseus.tufts.edu/cgi-bin/perscoll?.submit=Change&collection=Any&type=text&lang=Any&lookup=Aristotle
[139] https://ebooks.adelaide.edu.au/a/aristotle/
[140] http://remacle.org/bloodwolf/philosophes/Aristote/table.htm
[141] http://isnature.org/Files/Aristotle/
[142] https://web.archive.org/web/20050816192647/http://grid.ceth.rutgers.edu/ancient/greek/aristotle_greek/
[143] https://archive.org/details/aristotelisopera01arisrich
[144] https://archive.org/details/aristotelisopera02arisrich
[145] https://archive.org/details/aristotelisopera03arisrich
[146] https://archive.org/details/aristotelisopera04arisrich
[147] https://archive.org/details/aristotelisopera05arisrich

Article Sources and Contributors

The sources listed for each article provide more detailed licensing information including the copyright status, the copyright owner, and the license conditions.

Aristotle *Source:* https://en.wikipedia.org/w/index.php?oldid=864532627 *License:* Creative Commons Attribution-Share Alike 3.0 *Contributors:* A. Katechis Mpourtoulis, AlwayzaGentleman, Andrew Lancaster, Apcbg, Aristotele1982, Blanchette, BudapestJoe, Chiswick Chap, Chris55, Citizen Canine, DocWatson42, Dotoilage, Farang Rak Tham, Finnusertop, Headbomb, Holy Goo, JustAMuggle, Katolophyromai, Krakkos, MJV479, Mandruss, Mdanaher, Nicomachian, Omnipaedista, Rithme4, Rodneywang29, Ruyter, Sdc870, Spicemix, Tajotep, Textorus, Tim riley, Tkbrett, Witchofagnesi 1

Image Sources, Licenses and Contributors

The sources listed for each image provide more detailed licensing information including the copyright status, the copyright owner, and the license conditions.

Image Source: https://en.wikipedia.org/w/index.php?title=File:Padlock-silver.svg License: Contributors: AzaToth, BotMultichill, BotMultichillT, Gurch, Jarekt, Kallerna, Multichill, Perhelion, Rd232, Riana, Sarang, Siebrand, Steinsplitter, 4 anonymous edits 1
Image Source: https://en.wikipedia.org/w/index.php?title=File:Symbol_support_vote.svg License: Public Domain Contributors: Anomie, Fastily, Jo-Jo Eumerus 1
Image Source: https://en.wikipedia.org/w/index.php?title=File:Aristotle_Altemps_Inv8575.jpg License: Public Domain Contributors: User:Jastrow 1
Figure 1 Source: https://en.wikipedia.org/w/index.php?title=File:20160518_092_mieza_nympheum.jpg Contributors: User:Jeanhousen 3
Figure 2 Source: https://en.wikipedia.org/w/index.php?title=File:Aristoteles_Louvre.jpg License: Creative Commons Attribution-Sharealike 2.5 Contributors: User:Sting, User:Sting 5
Image Source: https://en.wikipedia.org/w/index.php?title=File:Modus_Barbara_Equations.svg Contributors: User:Chiswick Chap 6
Figure 3 Source: https://en.wikipedia.org/w/index.php?title=File:Sanzio_01_Plato_Aristotle.jpg License: Public Domain Contributors: Alan Liefting, Auntof6, Beria, Bibi Saint-Pol, G.dallorto, JMCC1, Jacobolus, Jarekt, Kentin, Mattes, MonteChristof, Sailko, Tomisti, Un1c0s bot~commonswiki, Wittylama, Wutsje, 5 anonymous edits 7
Figure 4 Source: https://en.wikipedia.org/w/index.php?title=File:Flute-player_dolphin_Alcesti_Group_MAN.jpg License: Creative Commons Attribution 2.5 Contributors: User:Jastrow 9
Figure 5 Source: https://en.wikipedia.org/w/index.php?title=File:Platonic_and_Aristotelian_Forms.svg Contributors: User:Chiswick Chap 10
Figure 6 Source: https://en.wikipedia.org/w/index.php?title=File:Four_Classical_Elements_in_Burning_Log.svg Contributors: User:Chiswick Chap 11
Figure 7 Source: https://en.wikipedia.org/w/index.php?title=File:Aristotle's_laws_of_motion.svg Contributors: User:Chiswick Chap 13
Figure 8 Source: https://en.wikipedia.org/w/index.php?title=File:Aristotle's_Four_Causes_of_a_Table.svg Contributors: User:Chiswick Chap 14
Figure 9 Source: https://en.wikipedia.org/w/index.php?title=File:DenglerSW-Stromboli-20040928-1230x800.jpg License: Creative Commons Attribution-Sharealike 2.0 Contributors: Steven W. Dengler 15
Figure 10 Source: https://en.wikipedia.org/w/index.php?title=File:Tremoctopus_violaceus5.jpg License: Public Domain Contributors: R. L. Hudson 16
Figure 11 Source: https://en.wikipedia.org/w/index.php?title=File:Two_of_Aristotle's_Growth_Laws.svg Contributors: User:Chiswick Chap 17
Figure 12 Source: https://en.wikipedia.org/w/index.php?title=File:Scyliorhinus_retifer_embryo.JPG License: Public Domain Contributors: NOAA 19
Figure 13 Source: https://en.wikipedia.org/w/index.php?title=File:Aristotelian_Soul.png Contributors: User:Chiswick Chap 22
Figure 14 Source: https://en.wikipedia.org/w/index.php?title=File:Aristotle_Senses_Perception_Memory_Dreams_Action.svg Contributors: User:Chiswick Chap 23
Figure 15 Source: https://en.wikipedia.org/w/index.php?title=File:Aristotle's_constitutions.svg Contributors: User:Chiswick Chap 26
Figure 16 Source: https://en.wikipedia.org/w/index.php?title=File:Bénigne_Gagneraux,_The_Blind_Oedipus_Commending_his_Children_to_the_Gods.jpg License: Public Domain Contributors: BotMultichill, Bukk, P. S. Burton, Wmpearl 28
Figure 17 Source: https://en.wikipedia.org/w/index.php?title=File:161Theophrastus_161_frontespizio.jpg License: Public Domain Contributors: Henricus Laurentius (editor) 30
Figure 18 Source: https://en.wikipedia.org/w/index.php?title=File:Arabic_aristotle.jpg License: Public Domain Contributors: Alarichall, Ashashyou, Chiswick Chap, GeorgHH, Ilse@~commonswiki, JMCC1, Joostik, Laurascudder, Orijentolog, Shakko, Urban~commonswiki, الدبوني, 1 anonymous edits 32
Figure 19 Source: https://en.wikipedia.org/w/index.php?title=File:Aristotle_and_Phyllis.jpg License: Public Domain Contributors: AnonMoos, Churchh, Jacquesverlaeken, Mattes, TeleComNasSprVen, Tomisti, TwoWings, Un1c0s bot~commonswiki, Wmpearl, Wst, 1 anonymous edits 33
Figure 20 Source: https://en.wikipedia.org/w/index.php?title=File:William_Harvey_(_1578-1657)_Venenbild.jpg Contributors: - 35
Figure 21 Source: https://en.wikipedia.org/w/index.php?title=File:Alexander_and_Aristotle.jpg License: Public Domain Contributors: Damiens.rf, Fatbuu, Grandiose, Infrogmation, Jonund, Mattes, Michel Hevia, Shakko, Tacsipacsi, Tomisti, Un1c0s bot~commonswiki, anonymous edits 36
Figure 22 Source: https://en.wikipedia.org/w/index.php?title=File:Aristotelis_De_Moribus_ad_Nicomachum.jpg License: Public Domain Contributors: Aavindraa, Chiswick Chap, Pasicles, Tomisti 37
Figure 23 Source: https://en.wikipedia.org/w/index.php?title=File:Aristotle_in_Nuremberg_Chronicle.jpg License: Public Domain Contributors: Chiswick Chap, JMCC1, Liondancer, Singinglemon, Tomisti, Un1c0s bot~commonswiki 38
Figure 24 Source: https://en.wikipedia.org/w/index.php?title=File:Gent,_Justus_van_-_Aristotle_-_c._1476.jpg License: Public Domain Contributors: Auntof6, Boo-Boo Baroo, Cathy Richards, Ecummenic, Faqscl, JMCC1, Léna, Mattes, Sailko, Shakko, Vincent Steenberg, 2 anonymous edits 39
Figure 25 Source: https://en.wikipedia.org/w/index.php?title=File:Lucas_Cranach_d.Ä._-_Phyllis_und_Aristotle_(1530).jpg License: Public Domain Contributors: BotMultichillT, Botaurus, Mattes 40
Figure 26 Source: https://en.wikipedia.org/w/index.php?title=File:Biblioteka_Marciana,_Aristotel.jpg License: Public Domain Contributors: BotMultichill, Ixtzib, JMCC1, Kilom691, Kokodyl, Mattes, MuMuTy, Oursana 40
Figure 27 Source: https://en.wikipedia.org/w/index.php?title=File:Turchi-AristotleIMG_1713.JPG License: Creative Commons Attribution-Sharealike 3.0 Contributors: BotMultichill, Bukk, Edelseider, Finoskov, Rvalette, Shakko 40
Figure 28 Source: https://en.wikipedia.org/w/index.php?title=File:Aristotle_by_Jusepe_de_Ribera.jpg License: Public Domain Contributors: Bukk, Hohum, JMCC1, Mattes, Multichill, Oursana, Pasicles, Zambonia 41
Figure 29 Source: https://en.wikipedia.org/w/index.php?title=File:Rembrandt_-_Aristotle_with_a_Bust_of_Homer_-_WGA19232.jpg License: Public Domain Contributors: Auntof6, Cobatfor, Ecummenic, Epidosis, Fæ, HBook, Jan Arkesteijn, Jane023, Paterm, Shakko, Slowking4, Vincent Steenberg 42
Figure 30 Source: https://en.wikipedia.org/w/index.php?title=File:Johann_Jakob_Dorner_d_Ä_(attr)_Aristoteles.jpg License: Public Domain Contributors: attributed to Johann Jakob Dorner the Elder (1741-1813) 42
Figure 31 Source: https://en.wikipedia.org/w/index.php?title=File:Francesco_Hayez_001.jpg License: Public Domain Contributors: BotMultichill, Bukk, Emijrp, File Upload Bot (Eloquence), G.dallorto, JMCC1, Kimse, Mattes, Pablo Busatto, Sailko, Shakko, Tomisti, Trockennasenaffe, 1 anonymous edits 42
Image Source: https://en.wikipedia.org/w/index.php?title=File:Wikisource-logo.svg License: Creative Commons Attribution-Sharealike 3.0 Contributors: ChrisiPK, Guillom, INeverCry, Jarekt, JuTa, Leyo, Lokal_Profil, MichaelMaggs, NielsF, Rei-artur, Rocket000, Romaine, Steinsplitter 47
Image Source: https://en.wikipedia.org/w/index.php?title=File:Speaker_Icon.svg License: Public Domain Contributors: User:Mobius 48

54

License

Creative Commons Attribution-Share Alike 3.0
//creativecommons.org/licenses/by-sa/3.0/

Index

Accident (philosophy), 15
Adaptation, 15
Aeolian islands, 16
Aesop, 29
Aesthetics, 2
Aether (classical element), 12
Age of Enlightenment, 2
Air (classical element), 11, 12
Alabaster, 1
Alasdair MacIntyre, 3, 36
Alberto Jori, 46
Alcmaeon of Croton, 21
Alessandro Turchi, 41
Alexander (2004 film), 37
Alexander the Great, 2, 4
Alexandria, 31
Alkindus, 32
Alpharabius, 32
Amyntas III of Macedon, 4
Anachronism, 39
Ancient Greece, 2
Ancient philosophy, 1
Andronicus of Rhodes, 6
Animal, 20
Animal behaviour, 37
Anna Comnena, 32
Ant, 21
Antarctica, 43
Antipater, 5
Aperture, 15
Apostolic Palace, 38
A priori and a posteriori, 7
Archimedes, 13
Archimedes principle, 13
Arete (moral virtue), 25
Aristoteles (crater), 43
Aristotelianism, 1, 2
Aristotelian physics, 2
Aristotle, **1**, 21, 22, 48
Aristotle for Everybody, 44
Aristotle Mountains, 43
Aristotle (Ribera painting), 41
Aristotles biology, 3
Aristotles Lagoon, 44

Aristotle with a Bust of Homer, 38
Aristoxenus, 31
Armand Marie Leroi, 3, 37, 44
Artery, 31
Asia Minor, 4
Astronomy, 16
Atomism, 31
August Boeckh, 49, 50
Averroes, 32
Avicenna, 32
Ayn Rand, 3, 36

Bee-eater, 20
Bénigne Gagneraux, 28
Benjamin Apthorp Gould Fuller, 45
Bertrand Russell, 3, 36
Biological rules, 19
Biology, 1, 2
Bird, 20
Birds, 20
Bivalve, 20
Body–soul hylomorphism, 21
Boethius, 33
Book frontispiece, 30
Boolean algebra, 3, 35
Botany, 4, 17
Bronze sculpture, 5
Brood size, 18
Bryan Magee, 30
Bust (sculpture), 5

Cambridge University Press, 45
Camera obscura, 15
Campaspe, 41
Carlo Rovelli, 13
Carpel, 31
Cassander, 4
Catfish, 17
Catharsis, 29
Catholic Church, 2
Catholic Encyclopedia, 48
Celestial spheres, 12
Cephalopod, 17
Cephalopods, 21

Cetaceans, 20
Chalcidian League, 1
Chalcidice, 4
Chalcis, 5
Chalkidiki, 1, 2
Chameleon, 20
Charles Darwin, 18
Charles Laplante, 36
Charles Lyell, 16
Charonia variegata, 21
Christian theology, 2
Cicada, 21
Cicero, 38
Cinema of the United States, 3, 37
Circa, 1, 2
Circulation of the blood, 3, 34, 35
CITEREFBarnes1995, 49, 51
CITEREFBloch2007, 50
CITEREFCarruthers2007, 50
CITEREFLeroi2015, 49–51
CITEREFLloyd1968, 49
CITEREFSorabji1990, 51
CITEREFTaylor1922, 50
CITEREFWarren1921, 50
Clarendon Press, 44
Classical element, 11, 12
Classical Greece, 2
Classical mechanics, 2
Claudius Aelianus, 49
Cockle (bivalve), 21
Collins English Dictionary, 49
Common descent, 18
Common fig, 21
Common sense, 21
Convergent evolution, 20
Cornell University, 51
Crab, 20
Critique of Pure Reason, 6
Crocodile, 20
Crustacea, 20
Crustaceans, 20

Dante Alighieri, 33, 34
De Anima, 25
Deductive reasoning, 7
Deliberative rhetoric, 28
Demetrius of Phalerum, 31
Democritus, 16
Developmental biology, 15
Dicaearchus, 31
Diogenes Laërtius, 48
Dithyramb, 28
Dolphin, 20
Duck, 18
Dunamis, 9

Early Church, 2
Early Middle Ages, 2
Early Modern, 3, 13, 34
Earth, 13
Earth (classical element), 11, 12
Economics, 1, 2, 27
Efficient cause, 14, 15
Electric ray, 17
El:Αριστοτέλης, 2
Embryo, 19
Empedocles, 11
Empire, 1
Empiricism, 2
Encyclopædia Britannica, 47
En:Digital object identifier, 45
English, 2
En:JSTOR, 45
En:OCLC, 44
Entelecheia, 9
Enthymeme, 28
Epic poetry, 28
Epideictic, 28
Epistemology, 7
Ernst Mayr, 31
Eromenos, 4
Esoteric, 38
Essence, 8
Ethics, 1
Ethnocentricism, 4
Ethos, 28
Euboea, 1
Eudaimonia, 25
Eudemos of Rhodes, 31
Eugene Gendlin, 45
Eurymedon the Hierophant, 5
Evolution, 18
Executor, 5
Exercitatio Anatomica de Motu Cordis et Sanguinis in Animalibus, 35
Exoteric, 38
Extinction, 18

Fecundity, 19
Felix Jacoby, 49, 50
Feminist metaphysics, 29
FGrHist, 49, 50
Final cause, 10, 14, 15
Fire (classical element), 11, 12
Fish, 20
Forensic rhetoric, 28
Formal cause, 14, 15
Formal logic, 30
Four causes, 14
Francesco Hayez, 38, 43
Fresco, 38
Friction, 12

Friedrich Nietzsche, 35
Frogfish, 17
Function (biology), 37

Gail Fine, 51
Galen, 34
Galileo Galilei, 3, 13, 34
Gas, 12
Gastropod, 20
Generation of Animals, 17
Genomics, 19
Genus-differentia definition, 8
Geoffrey Chaucer, 34
Geology, 16
George Boole, 3, 35, 51
Gerard of Cremona, 33
G. E. R. Lloyd, 44
Gestation, 18
Gestation period, 19
Government, 1
Greece, 1
Greek, 2
Greek language, 2, 34

Hagnothemis, 5
Hamartia, 28
Hans Baldung, 33, 34
Hare, 20
Harpalus, 31
Hectocotylus, 2, 17
Henry Babcock Veatch, 47
Henry Osborn Taylor, 44
Hephaestion, 31
Hermias of Atarneus, 4
Heron, 18
Herophilos, 31
Herpyllis, 4
Historia Plantarum (Theophrastus), 30, 31
History of Animals, 17
Homer, 16, 42
Hound shark, 17
Human nature, 27
Hybridisation (biology), 18
Hylomorphism, 8, 10

Ice skating, 49
Immanuel Bekker, 37, 51
Immanuel Kant, 6
Indiana Philosophy Ontology Project, 47
Inductive reasoning, 7
Interest, 27
International Academy of the History of Science, 46
International Standard Book Number, 43–46
Internet Archive, 48
Internet Encyclopedia of Philosophy, 47

Invertebrate, 20
Islamic philosophy, 33
Islamic theology, 32

James of Venice, 33
J. L. Ackrill, 44
Johann Jakob Dorner the Elder, 42
John Buridan, 2, 34
John Philoponus, 13
Jonathan Barnes, 30, 43
Jonathan Jones (journalist), 38
Judeo-Islamic philosophies (800–1400), 2
Jusepe de Ribera, 38, 41
Justus van Gent, 38, 39

Kinematics, 3
Kingship and the royal court, 4

Late Antiquity, 2
Laws of Association, 23
Lesbos, 4, 17
LibriVox, 48
Life expectancy, 19
Linguistics, 2
Lionel Robbins, 27
Liquid, 12
List of schools of philosophy, 1
Lives of the Eminent Philosophers, 48
Logic, 1, 2
Logos, 25, 28
Lucas Cranach the Elder, 38, 40
Lucretius, 31
Lyceum (Classical), 2, 4, 38
Lysippos, 1, 5

Macedon, 4
Macedonia (Greece), 3
Mammal, 20
Mantle (clothing), 1
Martin Heidegger, 3, 35
Material cause, 14
Material substratum, 8
Mathematical logic, 6
Mechanism (biology), 37
Medieval, 33
Metaphysics, 1, 2
Metaphysics (Aristotle), 4
Meteorology (Aristotle), 43
Michael of Ephesus, 32
Middle Ages, 2, 13
Mieza, Macedonia, 3
Milky Way, 16
Mimesis, 29
Mineral, 21
Misogyny, 29
Mnason of Phocis, 31

Mnemonic, 49
Mollusc, 20, 21
Money, 27
Mortimer Adler, 44
Movement of Animals, 17
Music, 1
Mustelus canis, 19
Myles Burnyeat, 45

Natural science, 2
Natural theology, 31
Neoplatonism, 2
Newtons First Law, 49
Nicomachean Ethics, 4, 7, 25, 37, 50
Nicomachus (father of Aristotle), 2, 4
Nicomachus (son of Aristotle), 4, 31
Nightjar, 20
Nile delta, 16
Nous, 25
Nuremberg Chronicle, 39

Octopus, 2, 17, 21
Oedipus Rex, 28
On Generation and Corruption, 8, 11
On the Soul, 2, 4, 21
Ontogeny, 37
Ontology, 7
Open Library, 48
Optics, 15
Organon, 6
Ottoman viper, 20
Ovoviviparity, 17
Oxford Studies in Ancient Philosophy, 47
Oxford University Press, 49

Palaephatus, 4
Paolo Veronese, 38, 40
Paper nautilus, 17
Papyrus, 2
Paradeigma, 28
Particular, 7
Parts of Animals, 17
Pathos, 28
Perception, 2
Pericarp, 31
Peripatetic school, 1, 31, 51
Persia, 4
Peter Abelard, 2, 34
Peter Medawar, 3, 36
Phenomena, 7
Philip II of Macedon, 2, 4
Philosopher, 2
PhilPapers, 47
Phronesis, 25
Phylogeny, 37
Physics, 1

Physics (Aristotle), 2, 4, 8, 13
Physiology, 15
Placenta, 20
Plant, 20
Plants, 21
Plasma (physics), 12
Plato, 2, 7, 10, 33, 46
Platonic Academy, 4
Platonism, 2
Platos Academy, 2
Plutarch, 51
Poetics (Aristotle), 2, 4, 28
Poetry, 1
Polis, 26
Politics, 1, 2
Politics (Aristotle), 4, 26, 27
Potentiality and actuality, 8
Potentiality and actuality (Aristotle), 9
Prior Analytics, 6
Private property, 27
Problems (Aristotle), 15
Profit (economics), 27
Project Gutenberg, 48
Proof (truth), 28
Property, 27
Protrepticus (Aristotle), 27
Proxenus of Atarneus, 4
Psychology, 1, 2, 21
Ptolemaic Kingdom, 31
Ptolemy I Soter, 4
Pulse, 31
Pythia, 29
Pythias, 4

Raphael, 3, 7, 38
Rembrandt, 3, 38, 42
Renaissance, 2, 34
Reptile, 20
Retail, 27
Rhetoric, 1, 2
Richard Sorabji, 44
Robert Drew Hicks, 48
Roman Empire, 5
Ruminant, 17

Scala naturae, 20
Scholasticism, 2, 33
Scrolls, 2
Sea bass, 20
Selachian, 20
S:el:Αριστοτέλης, 47
Sensorium, 23
Sexism, 29
Shark, 20
Shrimp, 20
Silver, 27

Skate (fish), 20
Snakes, 20
Social contract, 26
Solid, 12
Sophocles, 28
Soul, 21
Sparisoma cretense, 20
Speciation, 18
Speusippus, 4
Sponges, 21
Spontaneous generation, 21
Squid, 21
Stagira (ancient city), 1, 2, 4
Stanford Encyclopedia of Philosophy, 48
State of matter, 12
State of nature, 26
Stephen Halliwell (academic), 29
Stephen of Alexandria, 32
Stimulus (psychology), 21
Substance theory, 8
Suda, 4
Summa Theologica, 33, 51
Syllogism, 2, 28

Teleological, 20
Teleology, 31
Template:Aristotelianism, 2
Terence Irwin, 46
The Divine Comedy, 34
The Forms, 7
The Laws of Thought, 35
Theophrastus, 4, 30, 31
Theory of forms, 7, 10
Theory of impetus, 14
Therefore sign, 6
The School of Athens, 7, 38
Thessaloniki, 4
The tale of Phyllis and Aristotle, 33, 34
Thomas Aquinas, 32
Timaeus (dialogue), 7
Tinbergens four questions, 37
Trade, 27
Treatise, 4
Trial of Socrates, 5
Tufts University, 48
Types, 6, 49

Uniformitarianism, 16
Universality (philosophy), 7
Universals, 10
Utility, 27

Vacuum, 12
Validity (logic), 35
Vanishing point, 38
Vein, 31

Vertebrate, 20
Virtue ethics, 2
Viviparity, 20
Volcanic eruption, 16

Water (classical element), 11, 12
W. D. Ross, 47, 51
Western philosophy, 1, 2
Whale, 20
Wikisource, 47
Wikt:phantasm, 21
William Harvey, 3, 34, 35
William of Moerbeke, 33
Will (law), 5
Worm, 21
WP:LIBRARY, 47

Xenocrates, 4

Yolk sac, 19

Zoology, 1, 2, 30

www.ingramcontent.com/pod-product-compliance
Lightning Source LLC
Chambersburg PA
CBHW051350040426
42453CB00007B/498